Money Mindset Revolution

Transitioning From Nine-to-Five to Flexible Online Income

Angela Duval

© Copyright 2024 - All rights reserved.

The content contained within this book may not be reproduced, duplicated or transmitted without direct written permission from the author or the publisher.

Under no circumstances will any blame or legal responsibility be held against the publisher, or author, for any damages, reparation, or monetary loss due to the information contained within this book, either directly or indirectly.

Legal Notice:

This book is copyright protected. It is only for personal use. You cannot amend, distribute, sell, use, quote or paraphrase any part, or the content within this book, without the consent of the author or publisher.

Disclaimer Notice:

Please note the information contained within this document is for educational and entertainment purposes only. All effort has been executed to present accurate, up to date, reliable, complete information. No warranties of any kind are declared or implied. Readers acknowledge that the author is not engaged in the rendering of legal, financial, medical or professional advice. The content within this book has been derived from various sources. Please consult a licensed professional before attempting any techniques outlined in this book.

By reading this document, the reader agrees that under no circumstances is the author responsible for any losses, direct or indirect, that are incurred as a result of the use of the information contained within this document, including, but not limited to, errors, omissions, or inaccuracies.

Table of Contents

INTRODUCTION 1

CHAPTER 1: UNDERSTANDING THE TRADITIONAL MONEY MINDSET 5
   INFLUENCE OF SOCIAL NORMS IN THE WAY WE WORK 8
      The Family Setup 9
      The Role of Education 9
      Media and Cultural Influences 10
      Peer Pressure and Comparison 10
   WHAT'S INHERENTLY WRONG WITH THE NINE-TO-FIVE MODEL? 11
      Limited Flexibility and Work-Life Balance 11
      Risk of Burnout 12
      Job Insecurity 12
      Dependency on a Single Employer 12
      Limited Income Potential 13

CHAPTER 2: EMBRACING A NEW MONEY MINDSET 15
   EMBRACE THE DIGITAL ECONOMY 18
      Remote Work and Freelancing 19
      Entrepreneurship and E-commerce 19
      Gig Economy and On-Demand Services 19
      Digital Skills and Careers 20
   BENEFITS OF FLEXIBLE ONLINE INCOME 20
      Step 1—Self-Assessment and Awareness 22
      Step 2—Agenda Setting 22
      Step 3—Develop Positive Financial Habits 23
      Step 4—Embrace a Positive Attitude 23
      Step 5—Take Calculated Risks 24

CHAPTER 3: IDENTIFYING WHAT YOUR CURRENT SKILLS ARE AN WHAT YOU ARE PASSIONATE ABOUT 26
   TAKING INVENTORY 28
      Step 1: Self-Reflection and Assessment 28
      Step 2: Categorize Your Skills 29
      Step 3: Gather Feedback 29
      Step 4: Document Your Skills and Experiences 30
      Step 5: Identify Areas for Improvement 30
   ADJUSTING TO THE DIGITAL ECONOMY 31

CHAPTER 4: EXPLORING THE MANY ONLINE INCOME OPPORTUNITIES 35

E-COMMERCE 38
DROPSHIPPING 39
AFFILIATE MARKETING 40
DIGITAL PRODUCTS 41
CONTENT CREATION 41

CHAPTER 5: BUILDING A RECOGNIZABLE PERSONAL BRAND 43

THE IMPORTANCE OF A STRONG RECOGNIZABLE PERSONAL BRAND 45
BUILDING A STRONG PERSONAL BRAND 47
MAINTAINING A STRONG PERSONAL BRAND 49

CHAPTER 6: TRANSITION FROM NINE-TO-FIVE TO FINANCIAL FREEDOM 51

SETTING REALISTIC GOALS AND TIMELINES 54
FINANCIAL PLANNING 101 56

CHAPTER 7: DEVELOPING YOUR ONLINE BUSINESS STRATEGY 59

WHY DO YOU NEED AN EFFECTIVE STRATEGY? 60
   Clarity of Purpose *60*
   Audience Profile *60*
   Competitive Advantage *61*
   Think Sustainability *61*
UNIQUE VALUE PROPOSITION 62
A SMART BUSINESS PLAN 64

CHAPTER 8: MARKETING AND GROWING YOUR ONLINE PRESENCE 69

LEVERAGING SOCIAL MEDIA FOR AUDIENCE GROWTH 72
NETWORKING AND COLLABORATION 74

CHAPTER 9: MANAGING MULTIPLE INCOME STREAMS 77

DIVERSIFICATION 79
   Investments *79*
   Business Opportunities *80*
   Your Skills *81*
TIME MANAGEMENT AND PRODUCTIVITY 81
AUTOMATION AND OUTSOURCING 83

CHAPTER 10: OVERCOMING CHALLENGES AND STAYING MOTIVATED 86

STREAMLINE YOUR BUSINESS 88
   Resistance to Change *88*
   Financial Constraints *88*
   Skill Gaps and Learning Curves *89*
   Balancing Multiple Priorities *90*

    Building and Maintaining a Personal Brand 90
    Legal and Regulatory Considerations 91
   MOTIVATION DESPITE THE SETBACKS 92
    Overcoming Specific Challenges 93

CHAPTER 11: SUSTAINING LONG-TERM SUCCESS 96
   BE FLEXIBLE, ADAPT 97
   CONTINUOUS LEARNING AND SKILL DEVELOPMENT 99
   WORK-LIFE BALANCE 101

CONCLUSION 106

REFERENCES 110
   IMAGE REFERENCES 115

Introduction

Author and motivational speaker George Addair famously said everything you've ever wanted is on the other side of fear. You've probably come across this too, a common feature in personal development spaces. But what's it really about?

For most people, fear is often the main obstacle stopping us from achieving our goals and desires. Even before you attempt, you'll probably talk yourself down, asserting your fears. For example, you might see someone going over their preparation routine and think you're nowhere near as prepared as they are. Without realizing it, you just talked yourself out of that contest.

The mind is such a powerful thing, one of the most powerful things to be precise. You become what you tell yourself. If you think of yourself as a failure, certainly, failure will follow you around like a shadow. If you tell yourself you will face whatever comes your way boldly, you will always ooze confidence in everything you do.

Just so we're not encouraging wishful thinking, I'll be clear on one thing—thoughts must be accompanied by fitting action. Just because you think you're a conqueror doesn't mean your problems will bow down before you each time. Similarly, if you think of yourself as a failure, the thought in itself might not necessarily ground you. The resulting actions like not putting in considerable effort, not sending in that application because you believe so many people have applied already, or not taking a chance in whatever you'd have wanted to do. Your choices and actions stemming from your thoughts make all the difference.

So, back to Addair's concept of fear… to reach your full potential, you have to confront and overcome your fears. Whether it's fear of failure, rejection, or the unknown, Addair encourages you to push through because what's on the other side—your dreams, aspirations, and fulfillment—will always be worth the effort. The idea is that fear is a natural part of growth, especially when you're pursuing something meaningful. It's a part of life, just as failure is. However, fear should never stop you from taking action. If you're willing to face your fears head-on, you will unlock new opportunities and experiences that you may have never imagined possible. This is true because when you face your fears, you're challenging the false narrative in your mind that you're not good enough.

Treat it as heresy, and challenge it with facts—action! Sure, your circumstances might give you the impression that you're not good enough, but where are the facts? Now, if you decide to show up nonetheless, give your best, and succeed, you have evidence that you did it against the odds. At this point, you've successfully repealed that false narrative created by fear and replaced it with a can-do-it approach that will make all the difference in your life.

Let's talk about money.

Most of us grew up in households where our parents and other adults, maybe cousins, uncles, aunties, and neighbors were committed to their nine-to-five jobs. They left home early in the morning, braved the cold weather, and traffic, labored through the day, then braved traffic again to get home so tired that they could barely have the energy to do anything other than eat, sleep, and wake up early enough for the routine.

This is how the nine-to-five mindset was ingrained in us. It created the idea of security, especially job security. You'd get through school and hope to get a job where you labored through the same routine your parents did. This, for many people, is the idea of success, and we cannot begrudge anyone their wins.

The thing is, the world is changing, and tremendously so. We're a lucky generation because we're living through some of the most transformative developments in modern history. Look at cryptocurrency, changing the basic concept of money, decentralizing power and control over money, and taking away the control that central banks have always had. We're pushing the boundaries of space travel. We are tapping into the power of the Internet of Things (IoT) to create smart homes, and let's not even get started on the power of Artificial

Intelligence (AI). What a time to be alive! Throughout human history, great advancements have always been accompanied by a dynamic shift in the way we handle money, and our generation is no exception. Amidst all the transformations taking place, we're also experiencing a money mindset revolution, not only in how we make money but also in the way we work.

To embrace this revolution, we must first comprehend the need to switch from the traditional nine-to-five mindset to making money in this digital world. As with any new experience, there is always a strategy for setting yourself up for success. Since it's impossible to issue a blanket statement guaranteeing success, given varying circumstances, this book will give you a road map of the steps that you can take to set yourself up for success.

As we mentioned earlier, it's one thing to think about success, but without relevant action, it will always remain an idea in your head. The difference you seek comes from how well you can implement the strategies we'll discuss throughout this book.

Do you know what it means to challenge the nine-to-five mindset? You're challenging predictability. You're challenging stability. These are some bold assertions because, in essence, you are standing up to comfort. Most of us were taught to value this conventional approach, with job security and structured work hours being hallmarks of a successful career.

However, the digital revolution has introduced new opportunities and challenges, hence the need for a shift from rigid work structures to more flexible and diverse work models.

The rise of freelancing, remote work, e-commerce, and digital content creation has empowered people to explore alternative sources of income and work dynamics. Adapting to the evolving digital landscape is not merely about keeping up with trends. You have to learn how to recognize opportunity and thrive in a rapidly changing environment.

Your ability to adapt will influence your success, personal satisfaction, and long-term stability.

To help you adapt to the new money mindset, you will learn the following while reading this book:

- How limiting the traditional nine-to-five job model is, and how changing dynamics of social culture together with technological advancements are transforming the very essence of work.

- The fundamentals of the digital economy and various income opportunities that are available online.

- How to create a compelling personal brand and leverage social media to build a following and market your brand effectively.

- Effective strategies for balancing work and personal life, managing stress, and avoiding burnout. The goal here is to ensure long-term well-being and productivity.

In this book, we will explore various aspects of adapting to the digital age, from understanding new work models to developing skills and building a sustainable career. Whether you are transitioning from a traditional job, exploring online income opportunities, or trying to readjust your current work-life balance, this guide provides practical insights and strategies to help you through this transformation.

As the digital landscape continues to evolve, embracing change and adapting to new opportunities is key to achieving long-term success. My goal in writing this book is to show you how to navigate this process confidently, so you can thrive in the digital economy and create a fulfilling and sustainable career.

Chapter 1:

Understanding the Traditional Money Mindset

The traditional nine-to-five job mindset, that we learned from our parents, grandparents, or family, emphasizes a stable, structured work schedule where you work from 9 a.m. to 5 p.m., Monday through Friday. It was designed around job security, consistent income, and long-term commitment to a single employer. This is what most of our folks did, so naturally, it's the same path that many people have taken. This approach is commendable for the emphasis on hard work, discipline, and the belief that if you are to achieve long-term success and financial stability in your career, you must not only be loyal to your employer, but also be willing to persevere in your place of work, or your chosen career path.

If you grew up in an environment where the adults were committed to the nine-to-five, there's a good chance you've picked up a thing or two from them too. If anything, the nine-to-five mindset has been the pillar of modern society, a part of our work culture that has shaped how we work, our perception of employment stability, and the definition of success.

But where did this idea come from? Have you ever wondered why it works the way it does, or if something could be done to make it different, or better?

This schedule has been around since the Industrial Revolution. It was a time when factory work required a standardized schedule to maintain productivity and efficiency. This went on until early in the 20th Century when white-collar office jobs became popular. As more people picked up office jobs, the need for labor laws became apparent, and through their action, the eight-hour workday was formalized. With this formalization, anyone working the nine-to-five job model was considered a respectable, responsible, and reliable person, which was good for their social status.

The nine-to-five job model is built on three principles:

- Hard work: Employees were encouraged to put in sustained effort in their assignments. Hard work in this model emphasizes doing your work diligently and stresses the value of perseverance.

- Discipline: This is consistency in different aspects of the work routine, for example, following company policies, meeting your deadlines, and consistently following a structured work outline as proposed by your employer. Discipline is often seen as the cornerstone of order and reliability in the workplace.

- Loyalty: Anyone who's working the nine-to-five shift understands the relationship between loyalty to your employer and the promise of job security. Loyalty also means an unwavering commitment to the employer's values, success, and vision for the future. The promise of job security highlights the mutual trust between the employer and employee.

When you grow up around this structure, you are taught to believe that career success and financial stability are only possible if you commit to this detailed structure. An interesting thing about the nine-to-five mindset is the way job security is often associated with committing your productive years to a single employer and coming up the ranks until the day you retire.

Since our grandparents and parents went through this model and for the most part, we could see the benefits in terms of their ability to provide for us, it's fair to say that the family setup played a significant role in instilling this mindset. In your conversations with your folks, you've probably been encouraged to consider this way of life, with benefits like a retirement plan and health insurance being touted. Apart from the family setup, other influential voices like the media and our educational system have often consistently pitched the same idea over the years.

Let's face it, it's hard to not look beyond the trappings of the nine-to-five. For example, those who pay for their medical insurance out of pocket will tell you it's not the easiest thing to do. Therefore, it's understandable if you'd consider formal employment because your employer would assume this responsibility, and in some cases, include your dependents too. You might also be enticed by the fact that being formally employed makes it easier for you to access financial services like personal loans and mortgages than it is for someone who isn't formally employed.

The benefits aside, the nine-to-five mindset isn't without its quirks. For many people, lack of a clear work-life balance, stress, fatigue, and burnout are the unfortunate byproducts of following this lifestyle. Besides, as the world evolves, employers' needs keep changing, so job security isn't guaranteed anymore. Technological advancements, labor laws, and market dynamics have made it harder for employers to sustain the original promise of job security. Instead of job security, people have to contend with the inevitability of layoffs as employers figure their way around unstable economic conditions.

The rigid and structural nature of this work model has also been largely identified as a common reason for stifling creativity, the entrepreneurial spirit, and the pursuit of passion-driven careers. That being said, whether to follow this path or not, is a personal choice. You should, however, always weigh the pros and cons to ensure you choose a way of life that will not just take care of your bills and responsibilities, but also allow you to pursue your dreams and live a wholesome life.

Influence of Social Norms in the Way We Work

Everything we know about work has always been influenced by the society we live in. It's everyone from your family, neighbors, role models, and even random people you come across who might encourage or challenge you to do things differently. You might be at a crossroads, unsure of your next steps in life, until you listen to someone's success story and feel inspired to follow the same path.

The thing about society and the way we work is that there are lots of unwritten rules around things like career choices, work habits, and financial goals, often dictating what might be considered acceptable or the definition of success. These unwritten rules will always shape your perceptions and influence your actions in the work environment. When you join the workforce, everything from how you dress, the effort you put into your career, the social circles you join, and career milestones come down to the people you interact with. This is why it's a fair assessment to say society plays an important role in shaping your perception of work. Here's how that works:

The Family Setup

Your family or immediate community can be quite a powerful force in shaping your career path. Their expectations, implied or otherwise, inform the values and beliefs that nurture you from a young age into the working environment. For example, if you come from a family of successful politicians or attorneys it's almost certain that you might be nudged into a similar career path. On the other hand, if you grew up around entrepreneurs, you might be more inclined towards self-reliance and entrepreneurship than looking for formal employment.

The Role of Education

Our education system has for a long time been the catalyst for some of the career choices we make, and more importantly, conversations about work and money. Schools generally emphasize the importance of academic success in securing stable, well-paying jobs. In a way, the education system has for a long time encouraged students to pursue formal jobs, so much so that anything short of employment is often seen as an unconventional path.

We are, however, experiencing a major dynamic shift in this school of thought, with many schools encouraging and nurturing the entrepreneurial mindset in students. This comes from the fact that we have lots of successful entrepreneurs who have made significant strides in modern society, and who simply decided to break away from the herd and venture into uncharted territory.

Many institutions host such individuals to talk about their experience and show learners that there's so much more to life after school than looking for a job. The world is full of problems that need solutions, and therein lies the opportunities smart learners should explore.

Media and Cultural Influences

The media influences your perception of work in more ways than you'd imagine. Media and culture go hand in hand. Social media, movies, and television shows all help to create a certain narrative about work. For example, reality TV created a new brand of celebrities, and together with the power of social media, they created something glamorous, desirable to some, and a unique approach to fame for those who seek it.

Peer Pressure and Comparison

We cannot ignore the role of peer pressure in the decisions we make about our careers. It's only human to crave attention, and the desire to fit in. This explains why those who struggle to land jobs after school tend to withdraw from their friend groups, usually because they feel they don't fit in anymore, as everyone else seems to have landed a job already.

You might even feel pressured to pursue certain job opportunities or career paths so you can keep up with your peers. Unfortunately, this pressure to conform has seen a lot of people struggle with stress, anxiety, and even depression. The constant need to fit in can also lead to dissatisfaction, especially if your personal goals and values do not align with those of your social circle. This is one of those classic examples where your peace of mind and satisfaction become the cost of your success.

What's Inherently Wrong With the Nine-to-Five Model?

The nine-to-five work model is often criticized as flawed because it imposes a rigid structure that doesn't align with the needs of many individuals. This rigidity has in the past raised concerns over the effectiveness of this model, especially when we weigh the cost of productivity against the toll it takes on the personal lives of workers. This rigid approach assumes uniform productivity across the board, overlooking the fact that people have different peak productivity times and energy levels throughout the day. As a result, such a rigid structure easily creates inefficiencies, burnout, and a lack of flexibility in managing personal and professional responsibilities.

This rigid structure creates a host of problems for workers, most of which have a detrimental effect on their overall lifestyle. Let's explore some of these challenges:

Limited Flexibility and Work-Life Balance

One of the most significant issues in the nine-to-five job model is the lack of flexibility. It's a fact that the majority of the global workforce struggles to balance professional and personal responsibilities. You barely have time to complete all your tasks, let alone create time for yourself or your loved ones.

At times you carry work home at the end of the day, or during the weekend, yet you're supposed to be resting and spending time with your loved ones. It's no wonder a lot of people feel dissatisfied with their work, are stressed, and despite their perceived success in their careers, suffer depression and other mental health issues because of immense pressure.

Risk of Burnout

Working long hours with limited room for rest and recovery, intense pressure, and tight deadlines leave a lot of people predisposed to burnout. Work becomes synonymous with sustained frustration, which ultimately affects performance and has serious implications for your overall health and well-being.

The constant push to meet deadlines, achieve targets, and be productive even when the odds are stacked against you can leave you feeling drained and unfulfilled.

Job Insecurity

The job security that was once a promise of the nine-to-five model is no longer a guarantee. If anything, the job market today is too volatile for employers to offer this incentive. Economic uncertainty, coupled with rapid advancement in technology has pushed many employers to restructure their business models with an emphasis on cost-cutting, enhancing effectiveness, and streamlining their operations.

As a result, layoffs and job losses have become the norm, replacing the original promise of job security, even for those who have been loyal employees for years. Besides, the illusion of job security can make you complacent, discouraging you from exploring new opportunities or skills that could help you advance your career.

Dependency on a Single Employer

Relying solely on a single employer for your income is inherently a risky move. This is because you're assuming that the employer will be stable and equally loyal to you forever. Should the employer run into difficulties and have to restructure their operations, there's no guarantee that you'll survive the chop. Besides, when your entire career prospects lie with a single employer, your financial ability is limited, and you'll always be exposed to whatever risks they are exposed to.

Limited Income Potential

In a traditional nine-to-five job, your income is often capped by a salary structure that may not fully reflect your skills, experience, or contributions. Unlike entrepreneurial ventures or freelance work, where income potential can be limitless, a conventional job limits your earning potential.

This can be particularly frustrating for ambitious individuals, especially if you're at a point where you feel undervalued in your role. It's clear that for most people, the nine-to-five model doesn't meet the dynamic demands of the modern economy, where technology has made it easier for people to work from anywhere, at any time. Looking at the challenges unique to the nine-to-five model, it makes sense to explore other alternatives that could give you more freedom. In the next chapter, we build on this concept and explore a new money mindset that could transform your work experience.

Chapter 2:

Embracing a New Money Mindset

One of the realities of life is that change is always inevitable. Change forces you out of your comfort zone and once you get over the discomfort that comes with it, it might just be the most refreshing thing you've ever done.

In the previous chapter, we explored the traditional nine-to-five job concept that has defined the global work environment for generations and realized that even though it came with certain promises or guarantees, it's proven over the years to be quite ineffective and unfulfilling for many people. From a personal and professional level, so much is lacking in this model, and its demands have only resulted in a frustrated, demoralized, and often depressed workforce. If we keep going at the nine-to-five job model as it is, we might end up being one of the most depressed generations in the history of mankind. Thus, change is necessary. The good news is that a new perspective doesn't necessarily mean repealing the entire nine-to-five model, but a seamless integration. Welcome to the digital economy.

The digital economy represents a transformative shift in how we work, conduct business, and generate income. We're talking about the pervasive use of digital technologies to transform the way we work and live. Proof of this is the way the internet, mobile devices, and social media have changed our lives. Most recently, machine learning and artificial intelligence have hastened the pace of this transformation. Where the nine-to-five job model was right, the digital economy introduces flexibilities at different levels, creating new opportunities.

The digital economy isn't necessarily meant to replace the nine-to-five, but to support and streamline it, making it more efficient and fulfilling for all stakeholders. It doesn't take much to understand how important this is, especially if you cast your gaze back to the COVID-19 pandemic. No one would have imagined everything would come to a standstill as it did. The pandemic challenged the very core of the nine-to-five model, making it impossible for people to be physically present in their places of work.

Even though the pandemic forced many employers to urgently reconstitute their business models and allow remote or hybrid work models, the need for this flexibility has been apparent over the years, and many companies already had the models in place before the pandemic. We're talking about teleconferencing, webinars, and other structures put in place to help people work remotely. Most companies who had adopted this model primarily did so to alleviate the pressure on their employees and allow them to spend more time with their families. As this digital transformation effectively reshapes industries, creates new business models, and revolutionizes the way we live and work, we can see how the following characteristics not only support the digital economy but will be a mainstay in the future of work:

- **Connectivity and Globalization**: The digital economy has truly tapped into the power of the internet, living up to the global village tag it was once labeled. We're looking at more connectivity, allowing businesses and individuals to operate globally, regardless of the scale of their operations. Thanks to the internet, we can communicate and collaborate effortlessly across borders. This has made it easier to globalize markets, increasing competition and innovation.

- **Digital Platforms and Ecosystems**: The digital economy thrives on platforms like e-commerce sites, social media networks, and online marketplaces. These platforms are the pillars on which transactions, interactions, and the exchange of goods and services take place. They have facilitated ecosystems where businesses, consumers, and third-party providers coexist and interact, driving innovation and efficiency.

- **Innovation and Disruption**: The digital economy is a disruptor's economy. Most of the successful businesses have challenged the status quo. Look at taxi-hailing services like Uber vs. the traditional taxi business and rental arbitrage entities like Airbnb giving hotels a run for their money. The goal is not just challenging the traditional way of doing things, but offering the end-user value and a wider range of options to choose from, usually at a fraction of the cost they would have incurred in the traditional way of doing business. We've seen startups driving rapid changes in industries such as retail, finance, healthcare, and transportation, forcing established companies to adapt or risk obsolescence.

- **Data-Driven Insight**: We're living in the age of data. Since most of our lives are online, there are multiple points of interaction where we share data with businesses. From this data, they can draw valuable insight, making it easier to meet customer needs. Businesses leverage the power of advanced analytics, big data, and artificial intelligence to collect, analyze, and draw conclusions from vast amounts of information to make informed decisions. Data-driven insight has made it easier for businesses to enhance customer experiences, optimize operations, and drive strategic initiatives, giving a competitive advantage to companies that might have struggled to compete fairly in the past, especially against established brands.

Embrace the Digital Economy

The digital economy is the future of work. It's a timely convergence of flexibility and innovation, creating a work ecosystem that's conducive to creativity, greater autonomy, and a fair chance at a work-life balance compared to the nine-to-five model we've gotten accustomed to. The beauty of the digital ecosystem is the abundance of opportunities, particularly for those who can leverage technology to create value, whether through freelancing, entrepreneurship, or remote work.

What this means is that it's now easier for you to design your work around your lifestyle, create multiple income streams, and access global markets, hence an easier path to financial independence, personal fulfillment, and the power to make sure your work matches your values and passions. Here are some opportunities that have made it easier for people to thrive in this economy:

Remote Work and Freelancing

Work doesn't have to mean going to an office anymore. The digital economy has changed the concept of work, with more people embracing remote work and freelancing. With lots of digital tools and platforms available, you can work from anywhere.

This flexibility has allowed many people to enjoy the once elusive work-life balance. If you're a freelancer, you can explore global markets, offering your skills and services to clients worldwide without geographical constraints. The only things you might have to think about are how to align your timezone with your clients' and perhaps finding an appropriate payment method suitable for both contractor and client.

Entrepreneurship and E-commerce

The digital ecosystem has proven quite a godsend for entrepreneurship. Lower barriers to entry and access to online platforms have made it easier for individuals to start their businesses. This removes the usual bottlenecks to setting up a physical business, such as permits, licenses, and rent.

Today, e-commerce has grown tremendously, with many entrepreneurs tapping into online marketplaces and social media to reach customers and build brands.

Gig Economy and On-Demand Services

One thing you appreciate about the digital economy is how it continues creating opportunities and even industries that we might never have thought possible some years ago. The gig economy is one such example, a market of flexible jobs, usually short-term contracts. While this market has been around for years, its growth has been propped by a growth in the freelance mindset.

Businesses and contractors alike seem to be shying away from full-time employment in favor of short-term contracts. This is quite timely, given that the job security once promised in the nine-to-five model is no longer guaranteed.

Most people now prefer to devote their time to short-term contracts and pursue personal or passion projects when they're not contracting, as opposed to sitting in offices even when they're not productive. Platforms like Uber, TaskRabbit, and Upwork have been of great help to the gig economy, connecting clients and customers looking for on-demand services. This model has also made it easier for people looking for opportunities to supplement their income, or those seeking flexible work arrangements.

Digital Skills and Careers

As the digital economy evolves, the demand for digital skills continues to rise. We've seen emerging careers in cybersecurity, data science, digital marketing, software development, and AI, skills that are in high demand with advancements in technology. Acquiring and continuously updating your digital skills will go a long way in positioning you for lucrative and future-proof career opportunities.

Benefits of Flexible Online Income

A growth mindset, the belief that your abilities and intelligence can be developed through dedication and hard work, sets you up for success in the digital economy by championing adaptability, resilience, and a commitment to continually learning and getting better at what you do.

New technologies and trends emerge rapidly, and having a growth mindset encourages you to embrace challenges that come your way, learn from your failures, and persist in the face of obstacles.

This mindset drives you to seek out new skills, explore industry advancements, and innovate, which will be useful to thrive in a competitive and dynamic digital environment.

By viewing opportunities for growth rather than fixed limitations, you are more likely to seize new possibilities and achieve long-term success.

A growth-oriented money mindset, therefore, is essential in achieving financial success and stability.

Here are the steps you need to take to embrace this empowering mindset:

Step 1—Self-Assessment and Awareness

Begin by assessing your current beliefs and attitudes toward money. Reflect on your financial behaviors, habits, and emotions. Do you view money as a source of stress or opportunity? Recognizing your existing mindset is the first step towards transformation.

Examine your financial history and the experiences that have shaped your views on money. Consider how your upbringing, cultural background, and past financial decisions influence your current mindset. Understanding these factors can help you identify areas for improvement and growth.

Step 2—Agenda Setting

If you are to advance from the nine-to-five system and embrace the freedom that defines the digital ecosystem, you must change your thought process. We've seen how limiting the nine-to-five model is, and unfortunately, this rubs off on so many people. You can even think of it as being conditioned to approach life confined in a box. This conditioning, however, is not cast in stone. You have the power to get out of it, and transform your life completely, with a growth mindset.

A growth mindset champions the belief that if you apply yourself, diligently and consistently, you can achieve anything you set your mind to. New technologies and trends come up all the time, and with a growth mindset, you can embrace the challenges that come your way, learn from your failures, and grow even if the odds are stacked against you. The can-do spirit will surprise you some years down the line when you look back at everything you've achieved, which was once unimaginable.

With a growth mindset, you will find opportunities in places you might never have thought of earlier. You seek out new skills, explore new advancements in your industry, and are always looking for opportunities to innovate, which will be useful if you are to thrive in a competitive and dynamic digital environment. A growth mindset, therefore, is mandatory if you're hoping to capitalize on some of the benefits of the digital ecosystem that we've discussed. You'll soon realize that when you look beyond the limitations of the nine-to-five model, there are lots of opportunities for growth that you can exploit, seize new possibilities, and achieve long-term success. A growth-oriented money mindset, therefore, is essential in achieving financial success and stability.

Invest time in educating yourself about personal finance. Read books, attend workshops, follow financial blogs, and take online courses to enhance your understanding of budgeting, saving, investing, and debt management. Knowledge empowers you to make informed decisions and take control of your financial future. Be aware of the latest financial trends and developments. Understanding market dynamics, economic indicators, and investment opportunities will help you make strategic decisions that align with your growth-oriented mindset.

Step 3—Develop Positive Financial Habits

Develop a comprehensive budget that outlines your income, expenses, savings, and investments. A budget helps you manage your money effectively, prioritize your financial goals, and identify areas where you can cut costs or increase savings. Set up automatic transfers to your savings and investment accounts. Automating these processes ensures that you consistently allocate funds towards your financial goals, reducing the temptation to spend impulsively.

Cultivate the habit of delayed gratification by prioritizing long-term financial goals over immediate desires. This practice strengthens your self-discipline and helps you build wealth over time.

Step 4—Embrace a Positive Attitude

Embrace the belief that your financial situation can improve with effort and learning. View challenges and setbacks as opportunities for growth rather than obstacles. A growth mindset fosters resilience and perseverance, enabling you to overcome financial difficulties and achieve your goals. Surround yourself with people who share your growth-oriented mindset. Engage with mentors, join financial communities, and participate in discussions that inspire and motivate you to pursue your financial objectives.

Step 5—Take Calculated Risks

Understand your risk tolerance and make investment decisions accordingly. While it's important to be cautious, taking calculated risks can lead to significant financial growth. Diversify your investments to manage risk and maximize potential returns.

Accept that mistakes are part of the learning process. Analyze your financial missteps, learn from them, and apply these lessons to future decisions. A willingness to take risks and learn from failures is a hallmark of a growth-oriented money mindset.

While the digital economy offers immense opportunities, it also exacerbates the digital divide. Access to digital technologies and the internet is not universal, leading to disparities in economic opportunities. Bridging this divide is crucial to ensuring inclusive growth and equal access to the benefits of the digital economy.

We also have the persistent issue of data privacy and security. The reliance on data in the digital economy raises concerns. Cybersecurity threats, data breaches, and the misuse of personal information pose significant risks to individuals and businesses. Ensuring robust data protection measures and ethical data practices is essential.

Automation and AI-driven technologies can lead to job displacement, particularly in roles involving routine and repetitive tasks. Adapting to these changes requires reskilling and upskilling the workforce to meet the demands of new and evolving job roles. Governments, educational institutions, and businesses must collaborate to address these challenges. As much as the digital economy has created lots of opportunities, you must also be aware of the possible challenges you might experience, and plan for them adequately.

This smart approach will not only make your entry into the online money ecosystem smooth but also prepare you mentally to deal with the challenges that might come your way.

Chapter 3:

Identifying What Your Current Skills Are and What You Are Passionate About

What are you passionate about?

This almost seems like a question you come across in interviews, right? In that moment, your mind races through a number of scenarios, wondering if you have not just the right answer, but the appropriate one. Do they really care about your interests, or is this a trick question? What if you tell them what you enjoy, but it's not what they're looking for?

Well, that's the thing about interviews, you can never truly tell what happens next. However, the most important lesson is to give it your best shot. After all, the person who was there ahead of you might have done so, and the next one after you will most probably try to outshine you.

Away from interviews, the answer to this question is just as important when you're trying to find your footing in the digital economy. In a world that's awash with opportunities, the last thing you want is to commit your energy and resources to something that's going to drain your soul. Besides, if you start a business, prepare for challenges. There isn't a single business owner alive or dead, who succeeded in their venture without fighting some battles. This is where your passion shines through.

When things are rough, and they most certainly will be, your motivation to keep working on the business comes from your passion. Passion fuels your mission. It's where you draw the inspiration to keep showing up even when things are not working for you. Every business owner goes through such moments.

Therefore, when you're assessing your skills, one key aspect to consider is what you're passionate about. To determine your passions, ask yourself what activities energize you, even when they require effort or time. What are the tasks you find yourself naturally gravitating toward, or the problems you feel most compelled to solve?

For example, if you're passionate about creativity, you might excel in skills related to design, writing, or innovative problem-solving. If you have a passion for helping others, your skills might lean toward mentoring, teaching, or customer service. Passion often reveals itself in the areas where you are most willing to invest time and energy, even without immediate rewards.

Understanding your passions helps you identify which skills you are likely to develop further and which ones bring you the most satisfaction. It also guides your personal and professional growth, allowing you to focus on the skills that align with what you genuinely care about, leading to a more fulfilling and purpose-driven career.

Taking Inventory

Sure, you've figured out what you're passionate about. Now, of those passions, what do you excel at? To help you prepare for the cut-throat competition in the digital economy, it's wise to understand what you're good at.

Besides, your experience, talent, and skills will be useful in the next phase of your professional and personal journey, because once you branch away from the nine-to-five, everything is about you. Your brand becomes a part of your personal identity. In a way, you become the brand.

When you take inventory of your assets, you can identify your strengths, uncover areas for improvement, and align your capabilities with your career and financial goals. Here are the steps to effectively inventory your skills and experiences:

Step 1: Self-Reflection and Assessment

Begin by reflecting on your work history. List all the jobs you have held, including part-time positions, internships, and volunteer work. For each role, identify the key responsibilities, tasks, and projects you were involved in. This exercise helps you recognize the breadth of your professional experiences.

Consider the skills you have developed in various roles that are transferable to different contexts. Let's say you worked in a team before. Some of the skills you might have gained include project management, leadership, and active listening. These are transferable skills that are valuable in different job functions across multiple industries.

Review your professional achievements and accomplishments. Think about specific instances where you made a significant impact, exceeded expectations, or solved complex problems. Document these successes and the skills you utilized to achieve them.

Step 2: Categorize Your Skills

List your technical skills, such as proficiency in software applications, programming languages, data analysis, or technical writing. These skills are often specific to certain industries or job roles and are critical for performing specialized tasks. This might be a good time to highlight your soft skills. Soft skills like time management, adaptability, teamwork, and effective communication are always a bonus everywhere you go. They are necessary for effective collaboration and leadership in any work environment.

Include any creative skills you possess, such as graphic design, writing, photography, or artistic abilities. Creative skills can enhance your problem-solving capabilities and contribute to innovation in your work.

Highlight any managerial and leadership skills you have developed, such as strategic planning, team leadership, conflict resolution, and decision-making. These skills are crucial for advancing to higher-level positions and managing teams effectively.

Step 3: Gather Feedback

Reach out to colleagues, supervisors, and mentors for feedback on your skills and performance. Ask for specific examples of when you demonstrated particular skills or made notable contributions. You might not always be the best judge of your character, hence the need to gain feedback from external parties who have interacted with you in various capacities before. Go through your past performance evaluations and feedback from previous roles. These documents often highlight your strengths and areas for improvement, providing a comprehensive view of your professional capabilities.

Step 4: Document Your Skills and Experiences

Compile a detailed skills inventory that includes all the skills you have identified. Organize them into categories and provide specific examples of how you have applied each skill in your work. This inventory will serve as a valuable reference for job applications, performance reviews, and career planning. Create a skills matrix that maps your skills to different job roles or career paths you are interested in. This matrix helps you identify which skills are essential for your desired roles and highlights any gaps that need to be addressed through further training or development.

Step 5: Identify Areas for Improvement

Compare your current skills inventory with the requirements of your desired job roles or career goals. Where do you fall short? What skill gaps do you need to fill if you are to achieve your desired objectives? From this analysis, you will have better insight into your strengths and weaknesses, and identify areas where you can improve and focus your skills for the right development. Establish specific development goals to address your skill gaps. These goals should be actionable, measurable, and time-bound. For example, you might set a goal to complete an online course in data analysis within the next three months or to improve your public speaking skills by participating in a local debating club.

Adjusting to the Digital Economy

The global economy is shifting towards digitalization, automation, and remote work, so you have to adjust your skills and competencies if you want to stay relevant and advance your career. The traditional skill sets that once guaranteed job security are now being supplemented or replaced by new demands, such as proficiency in digital tools, data analysis, and adaptability to changing work environments. To position yourself strategically for these changes and seize emerging opportunities, you must actively update your skills and embrace a culture of lifelong learning.

Proficiency is no longer just about acquiring technical skills. Soft skills like emotional intelligence, creativity, and problem-solving have also become increasingly valuable. Employers are looking for individuals who can innovate, collaborate across diverse teams, and respond to challenges with agility. By continuously refining both your technical and interpersonal skills, you ensure that you can contribute meaningfully to your organization, adapt to new roles, and thrive in a dynamic, ever-changing economy.

From an employee's perspective, at times it feels like employers are asking for too much. Well, wait until you set up your business, and you'll come to understand why this is necessary. Customer needs, tastes, and preferences change just as fast as the job market is evolving. So in essence, it's not necessarily your employer asking you to bring your soft skills to the table, it's your customers who are demanding it.

Brands can no longer get away with treating customers at arm's length. They have to invest in the customer's purchase journey. Customers don't just pay for a product or service, they need more than your business offering. They need you to understand their story, so you get their perspective ahead of the purchase. This also explains why businesses that offer personalized products or service offerings custom-made to the customer's preference are thriving compared to those that generalize their business model to all customers.

What does this mean for you? As an entrepreneur, this is the time to align your passions with potential income opportunities that you might be interested in. If you love something and realize an opportunity to earn from it, go for it! This might turn out to be one of the most fulfilling and even sustainable career decisions you'll ever make.

In the nine-to-five, loving your work is something very few people ever get to do. Most people work because they need the money at the end of the month to sort their bills, not because they are enthusiastic about the job. Once you step away from the structured model, you have an opportunity to love what you do, enjoy it, and get paid for it. Your work becomes less of a chore, making it easier to stay motivated, especially during the difficult moments, and get you closer to success.

Here are some common income-earning opportunities that you can explore right away:

- Freelancing: Offering your skills and services to clients on a project basis, with common gigs including writing, graphic design, programming, marketing, and consulting.

- E-commerce: Selling products or services on platforms like Amazon, eBay, Etsy, or your own website.

- Content Creation: Blogging, vlogging, podcasting, and social media influencing. You can earn income through ad revenue, sponsorships, and affiliate marketing.

- Online Education: Teaching or tutoring students on various digital platforms. You can teach anything from academic subjects to professional skills and hobbies. As long as you are good at something, there's always someone willing to pay to learn from you.

- Affiliate Marketing: Promoting products or services and earning a commission for every sale made through your referral.

The list above doesn't exhaust the opportunities available online but gives you a good starting point. If you're trying to find your footing, especially if you're still new to the gig economy, you can always start with something simple, like blogging, writing articles, or data entry, or transcription. These are easier skills to learn, with low entry barriers. Once you get used to the flexibility and figure your way around freelancing, you can explore other fields, like customer experience or consultancy.

Whichever option you choose, be careful not to lose yourself in the pursuit of extra income. Always reflect on your values, passions, and interests to make sure that you are starting something you'll enjoy. Exercise your power of choice and do something that truly makes you feel happy and energized. Work to your strengths and natural talents and you'll have an inspiring experience.

Chapter 4:

Exploring the Many Online Income Opportunities

Having figured out what you're good at, or what you're passionate about, the next step is to find an outlet for your skills or talent online. It's no secret that there are lots of opportunities online. The question, however, is whether you can exploit these opportunities. Freelancing, for example, has seen tremendous growth over the years. Here are some of the major freelance platforms with lots of opportunities for remote workers:

- **Upwork**: A freelancing platform with a wide range of job categories, from writing and design to programming and marketing. You can create profiles, submit proposals for projects, and get feedback from clients.

Website: *https://www.upwork.com*

- **Fiverr**: Ideal for "gig" services, where freelancers offer specific services at set prices. You can create listings for your services, and clients purchase gigs directly.

Website: *https://www.fiverr.com*

- **Freelancer**: Similar to Upwork, Freelancer connects freelancers with clients through job postings and contests. You bid on projects and participate in contests to show your skills to potential customers.

Website: *https://www.freelancer.com*

- **Toptal**: This is for top-tier freelancers in fields such as software development, design, and finance. Toptal prides itself as a niche market compared to Freelancer and Upwork, hence the rigorous vetting process before onboarding freelancers, to ensure only the top talent is allowed in.

Website: *https://www.toptal.com*

- **Guru**: While this is a platform for freelancers in various fields, most of the jobs available are usually writing, programming, and design. Their workroom feature makes it easier to collaborate with other team members and handle various aspects of project management.

Website: *https://www.guru.com*

- **We Work Remotely**: This is a job board dedicated to remote work opportunities across different industries, listing remote job openings for roles in programming, marketing, design, and many more.

Website: *https://weworkremotely.com*

- **Remote.co**: This is another platform that lists remote jobs and resources for remote work. You'll come across job listings, company profiles, and remote work best practices to help you take the next step in your career.

Website: *https://remote.co*

- **FlexJobs**: This platform gives you access to curated remote and flexible job listings, including freelance, part-time, and full-time opportunities. To support you on this journey, you can access career advice and lots of resources to guide you through the job search process.

Website: *https://www.flexjobs.com*

- **AngelList**: This is a good platform if you're looking for an opening in tech companies and startups, especially those that offer remote positions. One thing about this platform is that you can learn so much about the culture of any company you're interested in, know them better, and use that information to prepare for your interview. More importantly, you apply directly to the hiring company.

Website: *https://angel.co*

- LinkedIn: LinkedIn prides itself on being a professional networking site that also features job listings. Companies usually indicate whether they're offering remote working or not, part-time or full-time gigs, so you can make an informed choice before submitting your resume. LinkedIn also has job search filters, networking tools, and access to company insights.

Website: *https://www.linkedin.com*

You'll appreciate the flexibility in choosing the kind of work you do, and your hours. With this flexibility, you are no longer tied down to a single employer, or industry. For example, you could run a successful consultancy as a legal expert, while at the same time creating content for your travel agency, or running an online store for pet supplies. Flexibility gives you an opportunity to diversify your income streams, which provides financial stability and freedom from relying on a single employer.

Even as you tap into these opportunities, you must assess each opportunity carefully to understand the time, resources, and commitment required to succeed. Remember, all options won't always be equally profitable, so you need to find the right fit for your goals and skills.

E-commerce

E-commerce is now an integral part of modern business, providing individuals and businesses a convenient way to trade in products and services online. E-commerce gives buyers and sellers access to global connections and looking at the growing number of consumers shopping online, you can easily respond to demand in a market where customers expect fast, easy, and secure transactions.

There are lots of e-commerce platforms you can explore for your business, with some offering a wide range of products and services, while others are niche platforms. Research well to understand the unique advantages and challenges of each platform before you invest in it. Ideal platforms should give you access to tools that help in managing inventory, payments, and customer interactions.

Perhaps, one important advantage of e-commerce over traditional brick-and-mortar stores is the potential for lower overhead costs. Your online store doesn't need a physical location, so you won't need to spend on things like rent, licenses, permits, utilities, and staff.

With these costs out of the way, you can focus more on scaling your business, marketing your products, and reaching more customers without the high costs associated with maintaining a physical space.

Dropshipping

Dropshipping is a popular e-commerce model where you sell products to customers without physically holding any inventory. Instead of purchasing items upfront, you partner with a supplier who ships the products directly to your customers once a sale is made. This means you don't need to invest in stock, manage storage, or handle shipping logistics, making it a low-cost way to enter into the online retail industry.

Since you're not meeting inventory management and handling costs, dropshipping requires minimal upfront investment. This makes it an attractive option if you're looking to test different product niches without the financial risk of unsold stock. You only pay for the products you sell, so you can shift your attention to marketing and growing your customer base.

While the absence of inventory handling is a good thing from an overhead perspective, it also creates quality assurance and control problems. You're essentially running a business off the goodwill of a third-party supplier, hoping that they will always fulfill your customer orders on time. This, unfortunately, won't always be the case. Any challenges on the supplier's side will always affect your business, and since you also have no control over shipping times, packaging, and product quality, things can get out of hand and escalate so fast. The key to success in dropshipping is to identify reliable suppliers who have a good reputation and proven track record, because if your supplier ever falls short of customer expectations, your business takes a hit, even though you bear no responsibility in the order fulfillment process.

Affiliate Marketing

Affiliate marketing is a performance-based business model where you earn commissions by promoting products or services from other companies. Instead of selling your own products, you act as a marketer for existing products, earning a percentage of the sales generated through your referral links. Similar to dropshipping, affiliate marketers earn without managing inventory, handling customer service, or dealing with shipping logistics.

This is one of the easiest online ventures to get into since you don't need to create or maintain products. Your emphasis should be on driving traffic to the merchant's website using unique affiliate links. These links track the sales or leads you generate, so you can earn commissions based on performance. Besides, you can promote products anywhere, from social media, blog content, email marketing, your WhatsApp profile and status, or even on your dedicated website.

Given the flexibility in the types of products and services you can promote, you are free to choose the affiliate programs that meet your needs on a personal level. Common affiliate platforms include:

- Amazon Associates
- ShareASale
- Commission Junction

Each of these platforms has a wide range of products you can promote, giving you the freedom to choose the best fit for your target audience or preferred niche. Remember, platforms and products that align with your interests, expertise, or audience, are always easier to recommend authentically than those that are outside your range.

Digital Products

Digital products are intangible items that can be sold or distributed online without the need for physical inventory. These include eBooks, online courses, software, templates, music, and digital art. The market for digital products grows with increasing demand for information and digital tools. This is why selling digital products is a scalable way to earn income with minimal overheads, making it an attractive option for entrepreneurs and content creators. This business model, surprisingly, has the potential for high profit margins depending on the kind of products you're selling. Once you create a product, it lives on forever and can be sold repeatedly without incurring additional production or shipping costs. With this level of scalability, you can reach a global audience and generate income continuously, even if you're not actively working. You don't even need to send customers the digital products yourself. You can simply create a link to the product, which is automatically emailed to the customers as soon as their payment is confirmed.

The beauty of digital products is their flexibility and creative freedom. You can create products whichever way you like, for example, by writing an eBook on a niche topic, building a mobile app, or creating design templates for businesses. Therefore, apart from monetizing your skills, you can also push the limits of your creativity and build a brand around your unique talent.

Content Creation

The idea is quite simple—create and share valuable, engaging material online. This is the ultimate creatives market since you can create content in different formats, for example, podcasts, videos, photos, articles, or even social media posts, for a specific audience. Content creation is a hit in online marketing because of the role it plays in building an online presence, driving traffic to websites, and engaging potential customers.

Brands rely on quality content to help them establish authority, connect with audiences, and ultimately monetize their effort through advertising, sponsorships, or driving direct sales. All this is possible because content creation makes it easier for you to build a loyal audience.

It's not just about creating material and posting it online, it's about consistently delivering relevant, high-quality content that can educate, entertain, inspire, or solve problems for your audience.

Quality content can also help you grow your audience organically because people usually share what they like within their networks, where they might have an authoritative voice. This is like word of mouth but on steroids.

Take note, however, that content creation demands consistency, creativity, and a clear strategy. With millions of content creators producing content daily, you might struggle to stand out from the crowd. This is why you should define your niche, understand your target audience, and create content that addresses their needs.

Chapter 5:

Building a Recognizable Personal Brand

You're walking away from the ultimate comfort zone—the trappings of the nine-to-five! This is a system so meticulously designed that all you have to do is show up. No one really cares about who you are, because the only identity that matters is your employer's. If you've been working for a company like Tesla, for example, most people don't even care who the marketing executives are, or the directors… but they pay attention when Elon Musk is speaking.

Now that you're moving away from this, you have to build your personal brand. You must be visible. People have to know you and relate to your work on a personal level. This is how you set up a thriving business. Over time, your success will gradually morph into a business brand, if you wish it so. Some people simply build the business around their personal brand, which makes things easier because your name is the brand.

Building a personal brand is important because, at this point, you are no longer housed under your employer's identity. The spotlight is on you, so you must get every step right. A personal brand also highlights the responsibility on your shoulders, because you are the face of the business and your future. This brand must, therefore, be unique and reflect your values, skills, experiences, and the things you're passionate about.

In a world where everyone's trying to run away from the nine-to-five, you can be certain you'll face stiff competition. Sure, you believe your ideas are unique, but there are many others who might have that idea already, that you might never come across. This becomes apparent when you start researching the business idea. That, however, should never stop you. There's enough room for everyone to make a living. What you must avoid at all costs, is copying someone else's work.

Given the stiff competition, you can be certain that some of your target customers already know about, or even do business with your competitors. Never forget that. You are not inventing the wheel, right? What will set you apart is your authenticity. The image you present to your customers, your persona, and your aura will set you apart from everyone else. It doesn't matter that your competitors might already be established brands in the industry. You just focus on what makes you better than them.

The good thing about venturing into a market with established brands is that they'll have done most of the research, so you simply need to track their steps. They also have disgruntled customers, so try to learn more about their frustrations, create solutions, and use that to build your brand. I remember some years back when the OnePlus phone was first released. It was touted as the flagship killer, a jibe at market leaders Apple and Samsung, who at the time, were often ridiculed for the astronomical prices they charged for their flagship releases. Today, OnePlus regularly releases flagship devices at prices almost in the same range as some Apple and Samsung models, but they already created an image in the minds of their customers that they're the flagship killer. So, diehard OnePlus users will probably not care about the price, because at the back of their minds, they believe they're getting a good device at a bargain. This is why you must be authentic when creating your brand. If you do it right, you get loyal customers who will walk the journey with you forever.

A strong personal brand does more than tell customers your story. It tells your story the way you want it to be experienced. This identity helps you convey a consistent message across all social media platforms and interactions, ensuring that customers have a carefully curated perception of your brand. In essence, it's up to you to tell them what to think about you.

The Importance of a Strong Recognizable Personal Brand

Whether you're setting up a business, a side hustle, or launching your freelance career online, a strong brand will take you places. This is your maiden foray into the entrepreneurship ecosystem, so you must get it right. A strong brand will get credibility and visibility. In your nine-to-five, everything was down to your employer's brand.

People knew their brand, logo, mission, vision, their community outreach efforts, and so on. They probably just knew you as Jane or John from the company.

For your personal brand, things are different. People MUST know you. Your reputation is directly tied to your brand. Your posts on social media and everything else about your personal life hinge on your brand. Wherever you go, your brand stays with you. This, therefore, is a good opportunity to establish yourself as an expert in your field.

If you do that, you make it easier for potential clients to recognize and understand your value in the hierarchy of their needs. It's quite simple—the more people know about you, the easier it is to attract opportunities. Put yourself out there. Join discussion forums and engage professionals and potential customers. These engagements help you create trust with customers. Your interactions with established brands and experts in the industry can also inspire your confidence, a reminder that you're heading in the right direction, despite the initial frustrations that all beginners go through.

It's a fiercely competitive world out there, so from the start, you have to think about differentiation. Make your brand stand out. You might not even need to do something drastic to get your brand noticed, at times all you have to do is listen to your audience, note their concerns, and provide tangible solutions.

This is one of the benefits of getting into a market where leaders are already established—everything you need to learn about your competition is already documented online through disappointed customers. If you do it right from the beginning, your unique qualities could help position you as the go-to person in that niche.

Personal branding gives you autonomy and control over your chosen career path. You're no longer operating under the banner of an employer. This means you can advance whichever way you want, and get all the plaudits for your effort.

There are no supervisors or managers taking credit for your hard work. If you choose to work long hours into the night and give up some of your weekends, you do it because it suits your plan.

A personal brand gets you a distinct identity which will be crucial in your career path, and your long-term success. Whether you're starting a business, setting up a consultancy, or freelancing your skills, a personal brand allows you to pivot across industries or roles, because it is all about you and what you can offer, instead of a single job title or industry.

The flexibility to work anywhere will get you access to opportunities for better financial growth.

Building a Strong Personal Brand

A successful personal brand doesn't happen overnight. It takes so much effort, and strategic planning to make it work. This brand should be able to communicate your unique value proposition and make you stand out in your field. As much as you're trying to appeal to an audience, this is all about you, so you must first assess yourself to understand what works for you. Identify your core strengths, skills, values, and passions, and determine what makes you unique.

From this knowledge, you can then figure out how your personal and business goals match your branding efforts. Let's say you're trying to grow a business or become a thought leader in your industry, how does this play into your career advancement goals? An appropriate match should bring forth a compelling brand statement that summarizes who you are, what you do, and the value you provide. More importantly, it should reflect your strengths and align with your goals. Building a consistent online presence is crucial for reinforcing your personal brand. You need a professional website to highlight your portfolio, achievements, and contact information. Think of this as your billboard, giving audiences all the vital information they need about your practice at a glance. Your website can act as the landing page. Create a professional social media presence.

Some people run their businesses on their personal social media pages. The best option will depend on the kind of business you're running, and your target audience. For example, if you set up a consultancy targeting backpackers, your life probably revolves around identifying hidden gems that would appeal to people with similar interests. In this case, there's nothing wrong with running your business on your personal social media pages.

Some customers will find this approach authentic and reach out for business inquiries. On the other hand, if you are setting up something like a legal practice or an investment consultancy, you might want to separate your business affairs from your social life. Whichever option you choose, make sure your social media profiles tell a comprehensive story of your brand identity, complete with professional photos and an engaging bio.

For all the effort that went into building your brand, it would be unfortunate to leave it hanging without quality content. Content is everything in the digital ecosystem. It's one of the biggest businesses in the attention economy. Create valuable, engaging content that people can easily share within their networks.

This gives you free marketing, and since people generally share content with trusted or close relations like family and colleagues, you're getting the best of word-of-mouth advertising working for you, and you don't even have to pay a cent.

Create a content strategy that can tell both your personal and business story. This fusion makes your content and brand relatable. Share insights, articles, and updates relevant to your business. Consistency is key in content strategy. It helps you create a schedule in the minds of your audiences and gives them something to look forward to.

Maintaining a Strong Personal Brand

You've laid the groundwork and set up a strong brand. Everything seems to be working well so far, you're getting quality leads and committing clients. Your next hurdle is how to keep this going. New competitors enter the market every day, not forgetting those who are already established. Maintaining a strong personal brand requires ongoing effort and consistency to ensure that your image remains relevant, credible, and meets your evolving goals.

One thing you cannot overlook is consistency. People expect it from your brand, otherwise, you'll lose your audience faster than you get their attention. Everything you do must present a consistent brand message. If you have a website, the content you publish must be consistent with what you post on social media. More importantly, update your content to ensure it remains evergreen, or you'll lose audiences who feel your content is stale. Life unravels every day, so you have no reason to keep the same post on your website or social media pages forever. Switch things up a bit. People need to see growth, so show it to them.

The fact that you've walked away from the traditional nine-to-five doesn't end your need for upskilling. If anything, this is the most important step you should consider boosting your brand. Attend conferences, take relevant courses, and engage in ongoing learning opportunities. The goal here is to try and demonstrate your commitment to growth while maintaining your position as a knowledgeable and credible professional. For example, if you are a computer programmer, knowing how to code in different programming languages isn't enough anymore. Today, you must also learn how to use AI or generate quality code with AI.

Maintaining a solid brand means constantly engaging your audiences. The core of these engagements is to build and maintain sustainable relationships. You created an image of a business that cares for its customers, so you have to maintain that, or the customers will walk away. People need to feel their opinions are heard and their presence felt.

If you can give your customers this experience, you'll have nothing to worry about. We're living in the age of data, so you cannot afford to ignore data insights. There are many points of interaction at which your customers voluntarily share their data. Use these to learn more about their preferences and purchase habits. As you understand your customers, it gets easier to present tailor-made solutions without necessarily charging them an arm and a leg. With tools like Google Analytics, social media insights, and surveys, you can assess what people think or say about your brand. There will be lots of areas for improvement, so take note and create a plan to address those issues.

At the end of the day, this entire process is about growth, so be ready to adapt your brand strategy based on feedback and changing trends, to ensure they remain aligned with your goals and expectations of your audience.

Chapter 6:

Transition from Nine-to-Five to Financial Freedom

The decision to pursue financial freedom through digital marketplaces together with, or away from the nine-to-five model is one of the best you could ever make, especially if we consider the abundance of opportunities available online. It's not just about choosing to do something different, it's primarily a seismic mental shift, challenging yourself to color outside the box.

You're moving away from relying on a traditional, fixed job for your income and instead choosing freedom in the way you spend your time and make your money. One thing you'll always appreciate about the journey to financial freedom through the digital ecosystem is that apart from financial independence, you also regain control over your life. Since you're no longer dependent on a single paycheck to meet all your needs, you can sit back, breathe a bit, and explore the endless potential of your income. This transition means something different for everyone, so from the get-go, I'll advise you to think about what matters to you. Why do you need the switch? What's not working for you in the nine-to-five model that will be addressed definitively by working online? This self-assessment is important because it not only gives you better insight into the kind of opportunities you can pursue online but also gives you a true sense of purpose.

If you've been caught up in the rat race, worried about how far you can go with your current nine-to-five income, worry no more. Creating multiple streams of income online takes care of this problem because you have a chance to break free from single-paycheck dependency. In the long run, you'll have saved and invested enough, or created income streams, to no longer need a full-time job for financial stability.

If you've ever had those random moments of anxiety where you're worried about what might happen if your employer closed shop, that's a thing of the past too. So what, if your employer lets you go? With the possibility of earning from different sources, you can reinvent your income through business, investments, or even set up side hustles. This is all about you.

A common complaint among those who have struggled through the nine-to-five model has always been lack of time. You barely have time for yourself, so you'll naturally struggle to create time for your friends and loved ones. The digital ecosystem can help you overcome this hurdle. You're no longer restricted to working a specific number of hours or being tied to your employer's office. You can do whatever you want whenever you feel like it. This might be a good time for you to revisit your passions, and hobbies, travel, or spend time with loved ones.

A caveat, however, is that this newfound freedom can be fleeting! Many have learned the hard way, that freedom, when abused, can easily ruin you. What am I getting at? Well, since you're free to choose everything from your work hours to the kind of jobs you pursue, there's always a risk that you might get complacent. Working from home requires discipline, without which your schedules and deadlines will start piling up, and before you know it, you suffer the very burnout you've been trying to avoid in the nine-to-five model.

If you do it right, however, you're on your way to living on your own terms. You can make decisions based on what you truly want in life rather than what you have to do to pay the bills. There's nothing wrong with continuing your nine-to-five either. You could keep it for the employer-boosted retirement packages and other benefits that you might not necessarily get directly from your freelance ventures.

If you love your nine-to-five job, perhaps it's something you're passionate about, or maybe you simply have an amazing team of colleagues, then you might not see the need to quit altogether. You can do both, and enjoy the best of the two worlds. At the end of the day, remember that this transformation is to help you do something you love, and not just because you need the money to take care of your financial obligations.

Now that you're clear on what you need, the next step is to plan. How do you get from point A to B? What must you give up? What do you need to support this move? Planning helps you ensure you'll be financially stable throughout the transition. This is particularly important if you're going cold turkey on your nine-to-five, quitting, and starting a new life online. The nine-to-five might have been a bore, but you were always certain of a regular paycheck on a specific day of the month. Since this might not be the case anymore, you have to think things through.

Approach this like a business. When setting up a business, you're always advised to have some money stashed away in an emergency fund. This should be enough to take care of your living expenses for 3-6 months, longer if possible. The goal here is to make sure that whether your new venture is making you enough money to support yourself and all your obligations or not, your life isn't grounded.

If you have loans, they'll keep getting paid on time, so you don't run into default. Your bills will be sorted, you won't lack food, and if you plan well, you might not even need to cut back on your social activities. By planning, you build up savings and budget for potential earning delays and gradually build your online business or freelance work to a sustainable level. At this point, you might consider walking away from your nine-to-five, so you don't spread yourself too thin, and instead, channel your energy to nurturing your new creation.

Depending on what you do, working online won't always be a walk in the park. Some people need to go through a learning curve before they get things right. Others simply plug and play like they've been doing this for years. Whichever the case, remember that everyone's running their own race, so don't be in a hurry to conform, or compare the pace of your success to someone else's.

The transition period gives you time to manage the learning curve that often comes with working online. The online workspace can be vastly different from a traditional office environment. You might have to learn new skills, how to use different tools, and implement new strategies. Preparation could be a resource-intensive experience, as you figure out the new skills, and online platforms, and set up the infrastructure you need to succeed, such as a home office or whichever equipment you'll need.

Setting Realistic Goals and Timelines

The plan is clear, so let's set appropriate timelines for the goals. What do you want to achieve, and when must you hit your targets? One of the challenges many people experience is getting their timelines right. Most people don't even have timelines to begin with. They wing it and figure things out as they go. Timelines are an important part of SMART goals, and without them, you might end up spending more time and resources where you shouldn't. Timelines create accountability, without which, your entire plan might as well be flawed from the start.

Start by assessing your current position and use that to set the blueprint for what comes next. Determine how much savings you have to support yourself during the transition period. We talked about the need for an emergency account to keep you going for a couple of months.

That's a good start, but don't stop there. If you can build the account to last you a year, that's even better. At least that way, you're always certain that if things don't work out, you can live on your savings for at least a year while you figure things out. As you work on this plan, it's also important to try and figure out the expenses you can cut out when push comes to shove. This should be a snap decision and also know the exact amount you'd be saving when you do that. What exactly are your goals during this transition process? Sure, you are moving from a nine-to-five, but what are you working towards?

What do you want to achieve in five years? What must you accomplish every year to get there? You need to build a resilient mindset, where you push your short-term goals and build on that progress to attain the long-term vision.

For example, if your goal is to start a new business, milestones might include conducting thorough research to understand the market, studying your customer demographics, creating a business plan, setting up your social media accounts, and building a website.

These are the small milestones you need to accomplish whose progress gets you closer to the ultimate goal. Remember, each of these milestones must have a deadline. This is good for accountability, and also to help you manage your time, so you don't end up spending more time than you need to on a single task.

Let's say you need to learn new skills to support your new venture. What courses should you pursue? How much will that cost? Do you need mentorship? The good news about courses is that you can learn so much online for free these days, so you don't necessarily have to enroll in a 4-year course.

Once you're certain the plan is complete, decide how to phase it in. Resist the temptation to implement wholesale transitions because if something goes wrong, you might derail the entire plan. Instead, start small and build momentum. If you're building a new business, start it as a side hustle.

This gives you time to test the waters and build experience without quitting your nine-to-five job immediately. Gradually scale up as you figure things out and learn the ropes. Monitor progress and adjust your plan accordingly based on your experiences.

Financial Planning 101

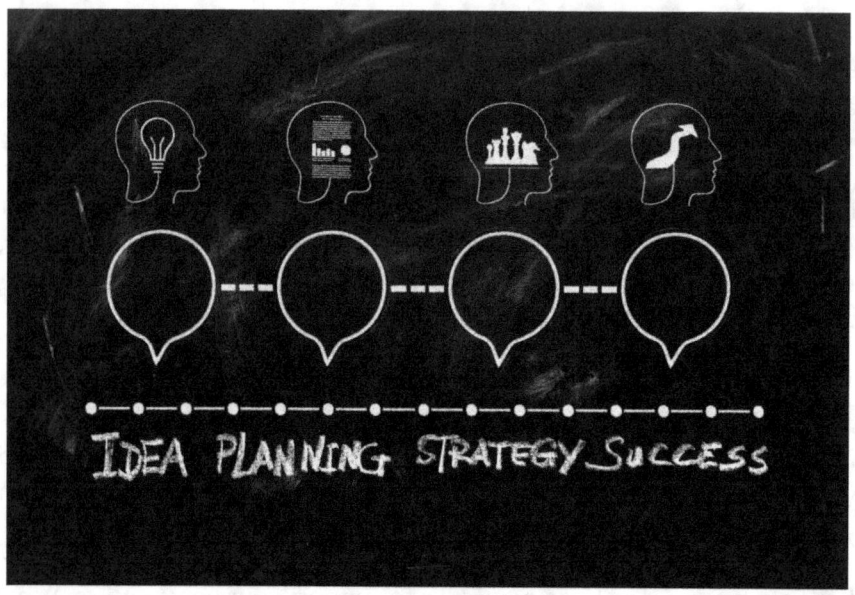

Let's talk about money! You're moving from a traditional nine-to-five with guaranteed income to online work, where your income will vary from time to time. In the early stages, most people don't make a lot of money. Some even consider quitting and going back to the nine-to-five they're used to altogether. Yet, those who soldier on through these trying moments usually get bolder over time. It's important, therefore, that you have a plan for your money during this tumultuous phase, so you don't make decisions you might regret.

You need a budget that accommodates the income uncertainty, so you avoid being in situations where you take on unnecessary debt, which will only stress you up further. The last thing you need in this transition is financial stress. Effective budgeting, saving, and expense management are crucial to ensure you can support yourself during the transition and set yourself up for long-term success. To understand your money and how it works for you, start by listing all your income sources, and expenses. This gives you a clear picture of what you're working with. From here, you can identify which recurring expenses you can cut off, and which ones to downsize.

Who has a claim on your money? This is where you assess your assets and liabilities. Assets are the things you own, for example, your savings accounts, investments, real estate, and any other valuable possessions. Liabilities, on the other hand, are claims external parties have on your money. You're looking at your credit card debt, loans, or even a financial promise you made to someone, which they intend to see you honor.

From this assessment, you now know what you own and what you owe. You now have sufficient information to build an effective transition budget. As you calculate the costs associated with this transition, some of the expenses that most people tend to forget include the cost of setting up your business, the cost of looking for a new job, the professional services you might require, and marketing. When it comes to financial planning, no cost is ever too small.

An important part of emergency planning is looking out for runaway expenses. It's quite simple: reduce unnecessary expenses or cut them out altogether. Identify and eliminate non-essential expenses. Focus on areas where you can reduce spending without affecting your quality of life significantly. Look for opportunities to negotiate lower rates on bills and services, such as insurance, cable, or internet.

Your expenditure at this point should be mostly on essential items, such as housing, utilities, and groceries. Ensure these are covered before you set some money aside for discretionary spending. You also need to plan for irregular expenditures. Think about the random medical bills, car maintenance, or annual subscriptions. Some of these, for example, impromptu medical bills, might fall under the emergency fund, but for things like car maintenance and subscriptions, you already know beforehand what you need, so create a plan for them.

Chapter 7:

Developing Your Online Business Strategy

Everything comes down to strategy. If you succeed, you must have had a good plan in place. If you fail, something probably went wrong with your plan, and you couldn't figure it out in good time. Alternatively, you probably didn't have a plan in the first place.

A good strategy will always be the beating heart of your success, especially if you're stepping into the digital marketplace. This is a market with stiff competition from individuals and companies alike, so without a good strategy, the odds will always be stacked against you.

A good strategy gives you a competitive advantage by building a business that's scalable from the ground up. This, effectively, is a business that's geared for long-term growth, and adaptable to the dynamic business environment.

Why Do You Need an Effective Strategy?

Here are some good reasons why you need an effective strategy for your online business:

Clarity of Purpose

Other than the fact that you're tired of the nine-to-five, or that you might just be trying to earn an honest living, what exactly are you working for? What's your vision for the business? What are your goals? A good strategy sets these out clearly so that your business effort aligns with a greater purpose. The business environment can be unforgiving at times, with things not working out as you'd imagined, customer preferences changing faster than you can adjust, and so on.

When such things happen, it's easy to lose yourself in the struggle, and even give up altogether. This is where your strategy sets you straight. Your purpose is a reminder that there's so much more to this business than the struggle. It's the kick you need up your backside when you're about to give up, that you have what it takes to rise up against the tough times.

Audience Profile

Many businesses fail because the owners don't understand their customers. Some business owners don't even know who their customers are. You cannot run a business by assuming you know what your customers want. You might know a thing or two about your competitors' customers, but that can only tell you so much. Besides, you don't know how your competitors run their business, so the last thing you'd want to do is assume anything. A strategy gives you the advantage of understanding their specific needs. With this insight, you can redesign your marketing campaigns, products, or services to address their needs accordingly. You're running a business in a world that's heavily reliant on data, so build a strategy along the same lines too. Your strategy should guide you on things like customer behavior, interests, and demographics to match your efforts with the right customers. This, ultimately, makes it easier for you to attract, convert, and retain customers.

Competitive Advantage

We've already established that the online ecosystem is a fiercely competitive environment for business. The question, therefore, is what sets you apart from everyone else? You're going up against beginners and established brands alike, so why should your customers ignore everyone else? A good strategy sets your brand apart from everyone else because it highlights your unique selling proposition (USP). If you're offering customers more value than they get from elsewhere, they'll choose you.

In a world of stiff competition, always try to offer value. If you're thinking of a business idea or a concept, ask yourself what value it adds to the lives of your customers. How does it make their life better? How does it compare to the competition in terms of improving your customers' lives? If your answers are affirmative, you're heading in the right direction. If not, figure out how to turn things around, and address the pertinent issues customers raise from time to time, and you'll certainly have a winner.

Think Sustainability

How do you get your products or services to the market? How do you engage audiences? How do you convert social media interactions to purchases? An effective strategy considers all these factors, making it a crucial component of any business. Your business must be built around sustainability, such that all your actions lead to something tangible.

You need so much more than sporadic marketing tactics. You should be able to track your campaigns, plan them in advance, and have an improvement matrix that enables you to learn from the success or failure of previous campaigns and use that to make bolder moves in the future.

Let's take your marketing efforts, for example. What kind of content do you need to create? How do you use your content to engage customers and build your reputation as an authority figure in the industry? How do you achieve better rankings on search engines through SEO? What strategies do you have in place for social media marketing?

Which strategies cut across all platforms, and which ones are unique to each social media platform you use? What's your approach to paid advertising? If you can address these questions in your overall business strategy, you'll have successfully created a sustainable plan for your business that can support your growth through different levels.

Unique Value Proposition

When building a business, you're often overwhelmed by the number of things you have to get right before the business gets going. You probably have a lot of questions in your mind, some of whose answers seem impossible. However, there are only two important questions that will always determine the effectiveness of your business strategy.

How well do you understand your audience? Given your answer to this question, how can your brand offer the value customers seek?

Your answers inform your unique value proposition (UVP) by addressing the real problems your customers are facing. An effective UVP represents the point at which your business vision, goals, and needs are met when you solve the specific pain points your customers struggle with. This is how you make your business indispensable, and your brand is the first thing that comes to mind whenever your customers need solutions.

To provide effective solutions to your customers, you must first understand their problems. This is where deep market research will be useful. Conduct surveys, and interviews, use social media and other online platforms to gather as much information about the said problems as possible. Go a step further and study your competitors. Sure, they might be established brands in the market, but there must be some people who are unhappy with their business model. Evaluate their concerns to ensure you are dealing with genuine discontent, and not malicious entities.

Since you already know the problem, show customers the solution. Don't just mention it and walk away, break it down for them. Show them the specific features of your brand that will solve their problem. How do you make their lives easier? How are the competitors ignoring their problems, and what steps are you taking to prevent that? What guarantees can you give them to prove that you won't ignore them as your competitors have done? After all, the established brands were once in your position and probably made some promises that they have been unable to honor.

As you engage potential customers, don't just tell them about the features of your products or services, show them the benefits. Tell them what your product or service will do to solve their problems. The goal here is to show your audience that your brand is relatable. Besides, when you communicate the benefits clearly, it's easier for customers to not only see the value but also realize that the brands they've been allied to have been giving them a raw deal.

Now, if there's one thing you must get right about your UVP is to keep it simple. It should be easy to understand at a glance. You don't want people confused, wondering what message you're trying to pass across. It needs to be succinct yet compelling, typically a short sentence or phrase that immediately presents the uniqueness of your product or service.

It should be clear, focused on solving a specific problem, and highlight the benefit your customers can expect while at the same time differentiating it from others in the market. Once that is done, test it with your target audience to ensure you're getting the intended feedback. Try A/B testing on your website, marketing materials, or landing pages to see which version of your UVP gets more conversions. Learn from customer feedback, and refine your messaging to make sure you're hitting the right spots. The goal is to make sure that your value proposition speaks directly to your audience's problems and evolves with their changing needs.

A SMART Business Plan

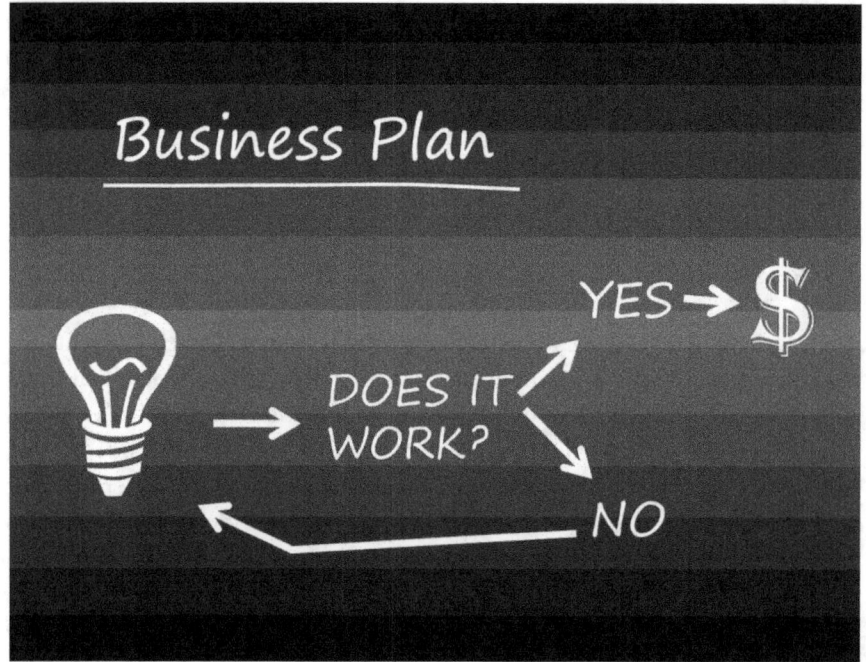

Your business plan can be the difference between success and failure. It is the blueprint on which the business is built, so you have to get it right.

A good business plan should feature SMART (Specific, Measurable, Achievable, Relevant, and Time-bound) goals.

Such a plan organizes your vision into a structured, and action-oriented strategy. If you do it right, your business plan should help you organize your ideas, secure funding, and execute your vision efficiently.

Since the business plan will be the go-to point of reference for your operations and strategy, make sure it has the following sections:

- Executive Summary: A concise overview of your business, including your mission, vision, and the unique value you offer.

- Business Description: A detailed description of what your business does, your target market, and your business model.

- Market Analysis: Insights into the industry landscape, competitor analysis, and market opportunities.

- Organization and Management: The structure of your business, including ownership, management team, and key roles.

- Products or Services: A breakdown of what you're selling, the benefits of your offerings, and any proprietary technology or features.

- Marketing and Sales Strategy: How you'll reach your target audience, your marketing channels, sales tactics, and pricing.

- Financial Projections: Forecasts of your revenue, expenses, and profitability over the next few years.

Once you have this structure in place, you can move to setting SMART goals to give your business a clear direction.

Make sure your business goals are specific, defining exactly what you want to achieve. Instead of vague goals like "grow the business," aim for goals that are clear and actionable. For example:

- Not Specific: "I want to increase sales."

- Specific: "I want to use targeted social media advertising to increase online sales by 20% in the next six months."

Specific goals remove ambiguity and set a clear focus for your efforts, making it easier to plan how you'll achieve them.

Building on specificity, make sure you can track your progress towards achieving the goals. Add concrete numbers or milestones that show you how far you are from the desired result. Measurable goals should include key performance indicators (KPIs), such as:

- Not Measurable: "Improve customer satisfaction."

- Measurable: "Use customer surveys to assess an increase in customer satisfaction scores from 75% to 85% within the next quarter."

Measurability is necessary to help you assess the effectiveness of the strategies you implement in your business.

Are your goals realistic? Take a moment and think about the resources at your disposal, your circumstances, and time. Do you think you can achieve the goals with what you have? While there's nothing wrong with being ambitious, setting the bar unrealistically high will only frustrate you. Even worse, you'll suffer burnout in the process. Instead of saying you want to gain 100,000 customers in one month yet you don't have a marketing budget, you can try investing $5,000 in targeted online marketing campaigns over the next six months to grow your customer base by 5,000. The point of achievable goals is to ensure you have the right resources and are using them effectively.

Your goals must be relevant to the business's overall vision of your business. It's easy to get distracted by short-term wins or trends that don't contribute to your long-term success. For example, launching a new product line that's unrelated to your core business just to follow market trends is not a good idea. It might feel right at the moment because of the hype, but it's not sustainable in the long run. If you want to launch a product, make sure it complements your existing offerings and addresses a customer need.

Finally, goals must be time-bound to create a sense of urgency and keep you accountable. Set a deadline or timeframe for each goal. Time-bound goals keep you focused and create room for structured planning. Instead of saying you want to increase website traffic, restructure this to using a targeted SEO strategy and content marketing to increase website traffic by 30% over the next three months.

With this plan in place, you can then break down the steps you must take in the three months to achieve the 30% increase, and possible adjustments if you achieve the desired goal ahead of time, or if you don't reach it at all.

Chapter 8:

Marketing and Growing Your Online Presence

Marketing your business online is no longer optional—it's essential. Every credible business owner today understands the need for digital marketing, mainly because most customers are online. To grow your business and stay competitive, you need to meet your audience where they are. Online marketing allows you to reach a wider audience. It levels the playing field for small and large businesses alike, giving them the same access to customers.

More importantly, it also gives customers prominence in the purchase journey through direct engagements with the brands they love. Without an online presence, you limit your reach to local audiences, word-of-mouth, or traditional marketing methods, which have proven quite expensive even for large, established brands. Growing your online presence is about more than just being visible. Sure, you'll get visibility and access to a global audience. What you do with this audience will determine whether you succeed or not.

Remember, bad news tends to spread faster in the attention economy than good news. If you're doing something good, people will appreciate your effort, but they won't make a fuss out of it, because they expect you to act right.

On the other hand, if things are not working for you, people will equally share your misfortune far and wide and even use you as an example of a failed brand.

To get the utmost value out of your marketing efforts, therefore, you must be intentional and strategic about it. Go beyond the allure of visibility, and instead, focus on building connections, trust, and authority with the audiences you interact with. Whether you're a business owner, a freelancer, or a content creator, quality engagement will always set you apart from everyone else.

Start by creating a clear brand identity. At a glance, people should understand who you are and what you stand for. What message do you want to convey to your audience? What's the first thing you need people to think about when they come across your brand? Think of this as your foundation. If you do it right, you'll never have to revisit it.

Engagement fuels the attention economy. Quality engagement comes from quality content. Your content is your voice online. It's the vehicle through which you communicate with your audience. There's a wide range of options you can use to drive engagements, from blog posts to creating videos or sharing images. Whichever of these you use, make sure it's something your audience enjoys, and will deliver your intended message effectively.

People find value in relatable stories. More importantly, everyone has a story, so share yours with them. Don't just wow them with your success story, talk about the struggles too. Be authentic, and you'll have an easier time connecting with your customers.

Customers generally seek connections with real people, not faceless brands. If you can weave storytelling into your content, you'll build stronger relationships with your audience. One thing you'll appreciate about online marketing is the way it gives you precision in targeting specific audiences.

Instead of a scattergun approach, create marketing campaigns that reach people based on their interests, demographics, behavior, or location. The beauty of this kind of targeting is that it allows you to spend your marketing budget more effectively so that your message reaches the right people at the right time.

In retrospect, this approach, compared to traditional marketing methods, ends up being more affordable and flexible. Why spend so much money on print ads, billboards, or TV commercials when you can run digital ads on Google, Facebook, or Instagram for a fraction of the cost?

Besides, you can also track performance in real-time and adjust your campaigns as your marketing needs evolve, so you get the best return on investment (ROI).

If there's an important point to take from this, it's the need to build trust with your audience. We talked about authenticity—customers looking to engage real people online. People interact with your brand because they feel they can trust you. They listen to your story and it resonates with them because you've created a connection with them at a deeper level beyond paying for a product or service.

Whether you send them emails, engage them in the blog comments, like and share their responses on your social media posts, make sure you interact with your customers, answer their questions, and use this opportunity to build strong relationships with them.

This level of genuine engagement creates trust and loyalty, and your customers will feel more connected to your brand because you listen to them. More often, people just want to be heard.

Leveraging Social Media for Audience Growth

Before you start creating content, understand who your audience is. Are they professionals on LinkedIn? Are you targeting young, creative users on TikTok? Would you wish to appeal to visually-driven consumers on Instagram? Every social media platform is unique and appeals to a different kind of audience. Your content strategy, therefore, should consider the strengths of each platform if you want to expand your reach.

Research to understand the kind of content your audience engages with. Content generally comes down to videos, images, posts, and infographics. Which of these does your audience prefer? With this knowledge, it's easier to create content relevant to audiences on each platform. Here's a brief guide on the kind of content that appeals to users on each of the major social media platforms:

- Instagram: Focus on high-quality visuals, short videos (Reels), and behind-the-scenes content. Use Stories to engage your audience with polls, Q&As, and interactive elements.

- Meta Platforms (Facebook): Long-form posts, community-building through groups, and sharing detailed articles work well. Facebook Live is also a great tool for real-time engagement.

- X (Formerly Twitter): Keep it short and conversational. X is ideal for quick updates, news, and engaging directly with your followers. Don't forget to use trending hashtags and participate in relevant conversations.

- LinkedIn: Share professional insights, industry news, and thought leadership content. LinkedIn is perfect for connecting with a business-focused audience through articles and posts that demonstrate expertise.

- TikTok: Short, engaging, and creative videos are key. TikTok thrives on trends, challenges, and authentic content that grabs attention quickly.

- YouTube: Longer, in-depth videos work best here. Tutorials, reviews, and educational content help establish authority in your niche.

If you're engaging audiences on more than one platform, make sure your message is consistent throughout. The content might be slightly different for each platform depending on your needs at that moment, but your brand voice, tone, and visual identity should always be consistent. Consistency builds recognition and trust no matter where your audience interacts with your brand.

Since each platform has unique peak times for engagement, research these and schedule posts accordingly. With tools like Hootsuite or Buffer, you can easily create a content calendar to ensure you're posting consistently, and at the right time. Remember, audience growth through engagement is just as important as content creation.

To grow your audience, try and build a community around your brand. Reply to comments on your posts, answer questions, and participate in discussions. This shows you're active and approachable.

Networking and Collaboration

In business, everyone needs someone at some point. Situations often arise where even those you consider your competitors will be useful to you. As much as you are trying to solve customer problems, you can't always have solutions for everything. This is why you should network and collaborate with other entrepreneurs. Besides, no one has a monopoly of knowledge of online business dynamics. Therefore, engage other business owners with the same zeal you interact with your customers, especially those business owners whose products or services complement yours.

Such engagements will expand your reach, give you access to new customer demographics, and increase your visibility and credibility. Competition is always stiff online, so building relationships with other entrepreneurs is in your best interest. It's a strategic move that introduces you to a vast network of shared expertise, and through combined resources, you could enjoy mutual growth.

Networking, especially with entrepreneurs in complementary niches gives you room to cross-promote your brand, creating a mutually beneficial situation for all parties. For example, if you sell smartphones and partner with someone who sells smartphone accessories, you can offer added value to your customers by sharing each other's content, products, or services.

You can cross-promote your businesses through guest blogging, joint webinars, podcast appearances, or shoutouts on social media. With the right strategic partnerships, you can easily grow your audience without using paid advertisement.

Beyond cross-promotion, your engagement with other entrepreneurs can also bring forth new products or services, creating a bigger value proposition to your customers than what each brand might have been able to offer independently. For example, you can partner with the phone accessories seller to create a smartphone bundle that gives your audiences the best value compared to buying the phone and accessories separately.

To this end, consider having joint product launches and bundle deals, or co-branded product offerings to help differentiate your brands from the competitors while giving customers a more comprehensive solution.

Working with other entrepreneurs can enhance your credibility and trustworthiness. When you partner with respected entrepreneurs in your niche, their audience will often consider you an expert by association. This assumption strengthens your authority in your niche and builds trust with potential customers who may not have been familiar with your brand.

Chapter 9:

Managing Multiple Income Streams

You're on the right path if you're setting up a couple of income streams. This is one of the best things about working online—there's no limit to what you can achieve. It doesn't necessarily all have to be online. For example, you could have some investments, a side hustle, some freelance contracts from time to time, or earn passive income like dividends or real estate. Whichever of these works for you, you're on the right track because you've essentially stopped relying on a single source of income.

In a global economy widely marked by uncertainty at individual and corporate level, relying on a single source of income can be quite risky. Anything that threatens the stability of your income threatens your very existence. As long as you have more than one source of income, you'll always have peace of mind, knowing that you cannot be grounded if one of your incomes is disrupted. This is also how you cushion yourself against unfavorable economic conditions, losing your job, or any unexpected financial hardship.

While having multiple sources of income is a good thing, it's equally important to know how to manage them effectively. You could easily burn through all your income and end up just as frustrated as someone whose entire livelihood is held together by a single paycheck. As much as multiple sources of income give you freedom, this freedom can be abused. You must, therefore, figure out how to make your money work for you without making some ridiculous mistakes that leave you worse off than you started.

The need to manage multiple incomes effectively is informed by the fact that this is about your growth potential. Once you start making lots of money, the only trajectory is upwards. Use the money you're making to create other sources of income or grow those you have already established… as they say, learn how to use money to make more money. There are endless opportunities once you start earning from multiple sources, so you have to be keen on how you manage your income. Remember, this is as much about managing yourself as it is about managing your money.

For example, many people succumb to the allure of lifestyle inflation. This is a situation where you unnecessarily increase your expenditure as your income grows. You probably move to a lavish neighborhood or a bigger house, buy another car, or upgrade the one that has served you diligently for years, you start eating at high-end restaurants, buy designer clothes, the latest gadgets, and so on. Your life suddenly gets an extreme makeover, and that's where all your problems start.

The more money you're making, the more responsible you must be to manage it effectively, hence the need for astute money management skills. If you're earning from different sources, you've probably figured out a creative approach to making money.

Similarly, that creativity will come in handy to manage your money. This can be both intellectually stimulating and rewarding, as it challenges you to continuously learn about personal financial management and take steps to protect your income.

The beauty of managing multiple income streams lies in the empowerment you get from it. It creates a sense of financial independence and resilience, giving you the freedom to live life on your own terms. The fact that you can ride out financial uncertainty while simultaneously chasing your personal and financial goals is a powerful and fulfilling experience.

Diversification

The value you get from diverse income sources is directly proportional to the strategies you put in place. Think of this from an investment point of view. You can't just buy stocks in different industries to shore up your portfolio. You must study the stocks and ensure that you're only adding stocks that bring value to the portfolio. Otherwise, what you'll have is a collection of stocks, not a carefully thought-out portfolio. There are three things you need to diversify to earn from multiple sources of income:

Investments

Have a look at your investment portfolio. Are you happy with the current composition? Are your investments value-adding or placeholders? Did you invest after careful research or were you swayed by the euphoria of a trend, and are now stuck with stocks that are underperforming, but you are too afraid to sell at a loss?

There's more to diversification than buying assets in different markets. You have to understand each market and its growth potential before you invest in it. Whether you're buying stocks, bonds, investing in real estate, or commodities, analyze each opportunity carefully to understand the value it brings to your portfolio, and from there, decide the appropriate weight you allocate in the portfolio. If you do anything other than that, you're flying blind, and your hopes will crash soon.

Business Opportunities

How is your money coming in? Sure, we've talked about walking away from the nine-to-five, but it's not mandatory that you do so. If you love your job, there's nothing wrong with keeping it even as you pursue other interests. If you're stuck in a dead-end job, you should think of walking away. At the end of the day, whatever job you're committed to should offer more value to you than the salary you get each month. What benefits do you get from it? How do the said benefits fit into your long-term financial plan?

Once you've figured out the employment conundrum, explore other possibilities. Why don't you set up a side hustle? The gig economy has lots of opportunities for freelancers, from consulting to specialized services and e-commerce, you can work anywhere. As you set up these gigs, think about how to turn them into passive income outlets. For example, you could create online courses, eBooks, or set up an affiliate marketing business. Anything that brings you money without demanding your daily active involvement should always be worth a try.

Consider part-time work. Many employers these days indicate whether they're hiring part-time or full-time, usually after weighing the pros and cons of each prospect, and more importantly, the costs involved. For example, it's easier for a company to hire you for a limited-time contract than bringing you on as a pensionable employee. As a contractor, the company doesn't have to contribute to your retirement account, so they save money on that front.

Your Skills

Now, the most important thing you should diversify is your skills. The more you know, the more versatile and in-demand you'll be. Learn a new skill today. It could be anything from online marketing, graphic design, carpentry, or computer programming. Think about something you might enjoy, go online, and learn about it. YouTube is full of free tutorials for pretty much anything you'd want to learn. Try supplementing your skills in a different industry. Think of services in a different industry where the skills you currently possess could be appreciated. This is one of the easiest ways to pivot or branch out professionally, growing your audience in each of the industries.

If there's one thing you need to be keen on, it's your digital skill database. Most of your interactions are online, from work to your personal life. With the growth in AI usage, this is the perfect time to improve your digital skills or learn new ones. There was a time when people would be concerned about being replaced by AI. That's no longer the case. If anything, the biggest concern at the moment is being replaced by people who know how to leverage the power of AI.

Time Management and Productivity

Time and money management go hand in hand. If you cannot manage your time, you'll probably struggle to make money. On the other hand, if you cannot manage your money, it's highly likely you are not so good at time management either. These two are valuable resources that we don't necessarily have in plenty. However, if you learn how to manage both effectively, immense benefits await.

You must be intentional about managing these resources to get the utmost productivity value. Without an effective management plan in place, managing multiple income sources can be overwhelming. It's important, therefore, that you learn how to prioritize key tasks and roles in your income-earning matrix, and never lose sight of your goals.

The goal here is to ensure that each source of income receives the attention it deserves. As much as you're working on different things, you shouldn't be spending a disproportionate amount of time on one while neglecting the others. Even if you have a full-time job, you can still create time for other opportunities. Besides, your desire to create multiple sources of income should not come at the expense of your personal life or overall well-being.

Let's say you have five sources of income. They won't always require the same level of involvement all the time. As we mentioned already, if you have a full-time job, it probably takes up the bulk of your time because you are duty-bound to your employer. Your side hustle, on the other hand, might only require a few hours a day, or checking in a few times a week. Given such differences in urgency, you should come up with a prioritization system to help you give each opportunity the deserved attention.

If you're at work, focus on your deliverables. If your side hustle requires two hours of your time every day, create that time, and eliminate possible distractions during that time. More often, prioritization comes down to figuring out which tasks to delegate or automate. If you do that, you free up your time from mundane tasks and focus on high-priority activities.

Productivity is mostly about routine and creating healthy habits around your work. What's your daily or weekly schedule like? How do you fit all your business and work roles in the week without giving up your personal time? You still need to rest, have fun with your loved ones, and engage in refreshing activities to avoid burnout. If you cannot create personal time, this effort might be in vain because there's no point working so hard to make so much money, only to spend it on hospital visits. For each income stream, set clear and manageable goals.

Have a tracking system in place to help you understand how far you've gone with each, and how much more you need to do. Whatever you are working on, be careful not to spread yourself too thin.

Automation and Outsourcing

Once the money starts rolling in, you should think about outsourcing some of the tasks or automating them where possible. These two are crucial for productivity because even though you might be handling things smoothly right now, it might not be possible as the business grows. Remember, you still need to pay attention to each of your ventures.

As you free up more time, you can explore other growth opportunities to earn more income and keep pushing toward financial independence. These two are powerful strategies that can also help you streamline each of your operations, cutting back on non-essential tasks to increase productivity. Besides, as you release some of these tasks, you free up more time for a better work-life balance.

Start by assessing the repetitive tasks. There are lots of apps, software, and systems in the market that are specifically built to automate such tasks. For example, for money management, you can easily automate your monthly contribution to your investment accounts, bill payments, or track your portfolio performance on platforms like Betterment and Acorns.

If you're in e-commerce, WooCommerce and Shopify are prime candidates for inventory management, order processing, and managing customer notifications. With these, you free up more time to focus on refining the core aspects of your business. You could also automate your marketing efforts using platforms like Mailchimp to manage customer engagement, send newsletters, and share information on new releases without necessarily sending each email manually.

You can also outsource administrative tasks like bookkeeping and content creation, especially if you don't have the skills. Content creation, for example, is the backbone of successful online businesses today. It's the foundation of every marketing campaign. People don't just interact with your brand, they appreciate relatable content. Your marketing campaigns don't have to flop because you don't have that creative spark in you. Hire a creative content designer to handle that part for you.

Even though automation and the need for outsourcing can be effective when managing multiple sources of income, they will never replace the value of your presence. Your businesses still need your personal touch. The key is to understand the roles and tasks that can be automated, and those that demand your direct involvement.

Chapter 10:

Overcoming Challenges and Staying Motivated

IM POSSIBLE

A growth mindset can be the game changer you never knew you needed. Most people never live up to their potential because of innate inhibitions. You pretty much sell yourself short, especially if you never try to explore what might exist beyond your comfort zone. The moment you walk away from the nine-to-five and seek opportunities in the digital ecosystem, everything changes.

You're venturing into the unknown. Your limits will be tested. Some people quit at the first sign of difficulty and run back to the familiarity of a nine-to-five. However, if you stay true to your goals, you'll understand that you must stick it to the end. Challenges are everywhere.

Even in the nine-to-five model, there are challenges every day you show up at work.

Therefore, it would be dishonest to say that the former lifestyle has fewer challenges. The only difference is that you are more familiar with the challenges, or your employer has an elaborate system for dealing with the issues as they arise.

If you put things into perspective, as a freelancer, for example, you are still serving the same clientele that your former employer was serving, if you remain in the same line of work.

Therefore, most of the challenges you might come across might be things you already know about, and how to deal with them.

Necessity drives creativity—this is why challenges will always be an important part of every entrepreneur's journey. Challenges will push you to go beyond the ordinary, think outside the box, and come up with innovative solutions.

When faced with obstacles like limited resources or intense competition, you are compelled to find unique solutions to differentiate your business from the competition.

This is also how your business grows. Each obstacle represents more than a problem that needs solving. It's something that drives you to refine your ideas, rethink some strategies, improve processes, or develop new products that meet the needs of your customers.

When you transition from a nine-to-five to the online business ecosystem, you're bound to encounter some challenges. Sure, everyone hopes for a smooth experience, but that's not always the case.

Transitioning to diversified income sources, whether by automating tasks, outsourcing, or adopting new business models, comes with its own set of challenges. Understanding these common obstacles and preparing strategies to address them can make the transition smoother and more successful.

Let's explore some of these challenges and possible solutions that you can implement to streamline your business processes.

Streamline Your Business

Resistance to Change

Moving away from a familiar nine-to-five job or established routine can create discomfort and resistance. People generally feel uneasy about leaving behind what they know. If you're in such a position, embrace gradual change. Start by incorporating new income sources or methods alongside your existing routine to ease into the transition. When setting goals, an incremental system will help to keep you accountable while building the momentum and confidence you need to thrive.

There's also the issue of uncertainty about the future and fear of failure, which have proven to be significant barriers for many first-time entrepreneurs. The unpredictability of new ventures can be daunting. Don't let it get to you. Every entrepreneur has been there before. A solution for this is to research the market. Do a deep dive to understand the factors unique to your industry, then use the insight in your strategy. Create detailed business plans, set realistic goals, and develop contingency plans. Small, calculated risks can help mitigate fear and build a sense of control.

Financial Constraints

The initial cost problem is evident everywhere you go. Most people struggle to set up businesses because they lack capital. Starting new income streams often requires upfront investment, which can be a barrier if your resources are limited. Instead of sweating over this, plan your budget carefully and explore low-cost or free options to set up your business. Consider bootstrapping or seeking small-scale funding options. Leverage free tools and resources to minimize initial expenses.

Once the money starts streaming in, managing cash flow can become complex when juggling multiple income sources, especially if income is inconsistent. It gets worse if you have no experience in cash flow management, or running a business.

A simple solution for this is to maintain a detailed budget and track all income and expenses meticulously. It's always advisable to create an emergency plan to get you through the difficult moments.

When you start a business, things won't always go your way in the first months. Some people even go more than a year before they can say they're earning an income from their new business. A good emergency fund will give you a fallback plan in case things are thick, so you don't have to dip into your investment to support your daily activities, like household bills and groceries.

Skill Gaps and Learning Curves

When you're transitioning to new income sources or business models, you might need to acquire new skills or knowledge depending on the business model you're venturing into. From the moment you decided to try your hands in the digital space, online marketing became a mandatory task. Every business owner today understands the fact that it's impossible to succeed without marketing your brand online. It doesn't matter how successful or famous you are, marketing is the reminder your audience needs to keep checking you out every day.

Even if you don't have the time or skills to do it on your own, you can still hire someone to help you with it. If you choose to go it alone, however, take your time and learn the basics. Gradually go beyond the basics, to learn some neat tricks and tips you can use to make your brand more visible online. You don't need to enroll in a 4-year course for this. Make use of online courses, workshops, and mentorship opportunities. Focus on incremental learning and practice to build proficiency over time.

We live in a world of new technologies, so adapting to new tools and systems for automation or online business operations will be an overwhelming experience for you. Luckily, there are lots of user-friendly tools that you can start with, and gradually move to more complex systems as you become more comfortable. Take advantage of tutorials, customer support, and community forums to ease the learning process.

Balancing Multiple Priorities

This is the jack-of-all-trades problem. As you continue diversifying your source of income, time management becomes an issue. The risk here is that you spread yourself too thin to the point where you can barely devote time to any of the businesses. Balancing the demands of a nine-to-five job with new ventures or income sources can strain time management and productivity.

If you're in such a position, consider prioritizing tasks and create a structured schedule. There are lots of management tools and techniques that can help you through this, for example, the Pomodoro technique, or time blocking. The goal is to stay sharp and maximize your efficiency. You don't even need to do everything on your own. Where possible, delegate some tasks.

Ultimately, it's possible that juggling multiple responsibilities can lead to burnout and affect your work-life balance. The last thing you need is to have entrepreneur burnout weighing down on you. Create a clear work plan that distinguishes personal time from work time.

Make sure your work hours are visible on your website, so your customers understand when you are available. When working, create regular break schedules so you can have some downtime to recharge. Implement self-care practices and seek support from family or mentors.

Building and Maintaining a Personal Brand

You need a strong presence for visibility and to grow your reach. Building a recognizable personal brand and establishing a strong online presence can be challenging and time-consuming. A solution for this is to develop a clear personal brand strategy and focus on creating consistent, high-quality content.

Audience engagement is about so much more than responding to their messages, it's about building a relationship. You don't know these people personally, yet you have a good opportunity to interact with them and make them your loyal customers. Social media has made it easier to build a rapport with customers, so much so that you might even learn how to personalize the services you render to each of your top customers.

In a way, this can also count as networking, because quality engagements with your audience often result in referrals and recommendations within their networks. Utilize branding tools and resources to streamline the process. Online business is about reputation.

Managing your online reputation and dealing with negative feedback or criticism can be challenging for a first-time business owner. Pay attention to your online presence regularly and address any negative feedback professionally and promptly. Focus on building positive relationships and providing value to your audience.

Legal and Regulatory Considerations

The laws governing online businesses are mostly still evolving, so you might encounter a bit of ambiguity from time to time. For this reason, navigating legal and regulatory requirements for new business ventures or income sources can be complex.

Try to research and understand the legal requirements for your new income sources. Consult with legal and financial professionals to ensure compliance with regulations and to handle contracts, taxes, and other legal matters.

One of the biggest challenges you'll come across here is the issue of intellectual property (IP). Protecting your intellectual property (IP) such as digital products, content, or brand assets is important, but at the same time, a tricky affair if you don't know how to go about it.

Engage your attorney to advise you on how to register trademarks, copyrights, or patents as needed to protect your IP. Use legal agreements and contracts to safeguard your work and ideas.

Motivation Despite the Setbacks

We learn from our mistakes, and that's how growth comes about. Never run away from setbacks. Instead, be brave and face them head-on. The lessons you learn through these experiences make you bolder, more resilient, and more motivated to keep working towards your goals. Whether in your personal life or running your business, setbacks will always be a normal part of the learning curve. Common setbacks can range from unexpected financial issues, technical difficulties, or sudden changes in market conditions that disrupt progress.

Additionally, early failures or underperformance compared to expectations can lead to discouragement. On a more personal level, obstacles like health issues, personal conflicts, or burnout can significantly impact one's ability to remain focused and motivated. Understanding these setbacks is crucial for maintaining resilience. Instead of viewing setbacks as indicators of failure, it's important to reframe them as learning opportunities.

When things don't work out as you had planned, take a step back and figure out why. Did you miss anything? Did you assume something crucial? Did someone not come through for you? Were the odds simply stacked against you, for example, the state of the economy or the seasons simply could not sustain your concept?

These moments of introspection can help you identify areas where you can make some changes and come back stronger. Apart from that, your insight from such moments could also provide useful strategic action points for future activity. This approach helps transform what might initially seem like a defeat into a stepping stone for growth.

Overcoming Specific Challenges

Facing financial setbacks requires careful planning and resource management. One of the first things every entrepreneur does is to create a budget relevant to their financial situation. This will go a long way in managing your resources effectively and prepare you to handle unexpected expenses. Even with a budget, you still can never be too prepared for what life throws at you.

For that reason, create a failsafe, a backup plan that can help you in case you run into unmitigated funding issues. For example, if that bank loan you were counting on doesn't come through, what happens? You definitely aren't planning on closing the shop, right? Being proactive in your financial planning can mitigate the impact of setbacks and keep your goals on track.

When dealing with financial difficulties, seeking support is crucial. Reach out to financial advisors, mentors, or peers for advice and guidance. They can offer valuable insights and help you navigate the complexities of financial challenges. Whether it's restructuring your budget or finding new revenue streams, having a support system in place ensures that you're not facing these obstacles alone.

Technical difficulties can disrupt progress, but they can often be resolved with the right approach. Begin by troubleshooting the issues and dedicating time to learning the tools or technologies causing the problems.

Staying informed about the latest technological developments can prevent future challenges and improve your overall efficiency. When the issue is beyond your expertise, don't hesitate to utilize customer support, online communities, or even hire experts to resolve the problem swiftly and effectively.

Performance issues, whether in business or personal projects, require a strategic approach to improvement. Start by analyzing performance data to pinpoint areas that need enhancement. This analysis will provide you with insights that can guide your strategy adjustments. Additionally, seeking feedback from customers, peers, or mentors is essential to understanding the root causes of performance issues. By incorporating their suggestions and making the necessary adjustments, you can enhance your performance and move closer to your goals.

Chapter 11:

Sustaining Long-Term Success

When it comes to your money, always think long-term. A long-term plan allows you to make adjustments where necessary and will include some short-term plans, which we'll call milestones. Think of milestones like items on your to-do list. Each item you check off the list gets you closer to accomplishing your ultimate objective. The same applies to milestones.

If you say you want a bank balance of $100,000 ten years from now, a smart approach would be breaking this plan into phases, say three years each. How much must you have in your account at the end of the first and subsequent three-year cycles? Now, break down each 3-year cycle into annual reviews.

For each annual review, have a quarterly or monthly target. Depending on your circumstances, you might even go further and have weekly targets that build into the month, the quarter, the annual review, the three-year target, and ultimately, your plan becomes a success at the end of year 10. This is how milestones work. Milestones eliminate ambiguity from your plans and keep you accountable throughout. More importantly, each milestone you accomplish gives you the drive to go harder, and if you keep it up, you might even achieve your long-term goals in a shorter time.

Besides, you also have the compounding effect of money working for you, so if you stay the course, there's a good chance you might have $100,000 in your account somewhere between years seven and nine, especially if your financial situation improves along the way, and you adjust your contributions upwards.

Be Flexible, Adapt

If there's one thing we've learned about the internet and life in general, it's the fact that change is inevitable. You either adapt or perish. Google and Gmail thrive today, synonymous with search engines and emails. Yet, Bing and Yahoo were once industry leaders in this sector.

Most people use the Google Docs suite for documents, yet there was a time when Microsoft Office Suite was the ultimate document processor. What we have here is proof that you must not only adapt but be aware of the reality that in the internet age, nothing and no one is too big to fall.

For your businesses and financial plans, be flexible. Pay attention to what's happening around you, and more importantly, be receptive to new knowledge. The last thing you want to be in such a dynamic space is obsolete, or investing in dead-end projects. You must always adapt.

That's the only way to position yourself for success. Whether you're looking at investment opportunities or business ideas, changes in the digital ecosystem are rapid, and customer behavior and preferences are more dynamic than ever, especially if you factor in how social media drives FOMO (fear of missing out).

You cannot ignore the internet anymore. Woe unto you if you think otherwise. Embrace the digital economy fully, because this is where the new economic revolution will take place. We've seen how blockchain technology has transformed the traditional financial sector and digital wallets challenging stalwarts like third-party payment processors.

Be keen on emerging technologies because their impact is swift and immediate. Look at blockchain, virtual reality, machine learning, and artificial intelligence, and how they can fit into your financial plans. As they reshape the online landscape, so should you refine your strategies.

Don't just learn about these advancements, find out how to gain a competitive advantage with them. Whichever platform you're using, keep an eye out for the algorithm and feature updates, because some updates could make your strategies obsolete overnight.

If you're running a business, monitor evolving customer behavior and preferences. One unique trait about customers in the internet age is that their opinions are so easy to sway. More often, all it takes is an influencer's voice. Some customers might not even care about the utility value they derive from your business, product, or service, as long as they have the trendy item pitched by their favorite influencer. At times it comes down to what's trending at the moment, and not necessarily about what's useful.

It's a highly competitive market, so you must also understand its core dynamics. Who are the new entrants and what's their value proposition? Given the fierce competition, how are the established companies holding onto their market share?

What are they doing differently to stay ahead of everyone else? How's the competition shifting from time to time? What complementary or supplementary products or services are in the market, and how do they affect your position? Your answers to these questions will influence your approach and strategy for sustainable long-term success.

Adaptation is about relevance. Don't allow change to outpace you. Given how fast things change today, if you don't adjust and adapt promptly, you might never recover or regain your space in the market. Customers move on swiftly, don't let them move on without you!

Continuous Learning and Skill Development

If you're going to build a business or strategies that can adapt to changing business dynamics, you must also be willing to learn and upskill. From job requirements to technological advancements and industry dynamics, upskilling keeps you relevant and competitive. Platforms and the tools you use in your business are updated all the time, and some are replaced altogether. Roles and skills also change all the time, so the point of ongoing education is to help you keep up with industry demands.

Even if you're not in the business sector, think about your career prospects. New skills and knowledge broaden your expertise and strengthen your candidacy when presented with new career opportunities. There's always room for growth, whether in a personal or professional capacity.

The more you pursue growth opportunities, the more valuable you become to your employers and clients because they want to be a part of your growth. Your commitment to continuous learning also puts you in a unique position to manage change.

As things evolve around you, there's always a chance that the changes might not go down well with everyone. People have different visions in life, so some changes might not be readily welcome, even though they are necessary. In such cases, your ability to manage such situations effectively, bridge the gap, and bring everyone on board, could be the difference between success and failure. The goal here is to champion innovation, not just in the result, but also in the processes and the people who are responsible for the desired results.

So, how do you prepare yourself for such a dynamic experience?

The first step is to understand where you're coming from, and what you are working towards. Make sure you're working towards something that adds value to your life in different capacities. If your goal is a $100,000 bank balance in 10 years, ask yourself why this particular amount matters to you. Why not $80,000 or $150,000? What's so unique about $100,000? Put meaning to your goals, because this is where you derive motivation when you're going through a rough patch.

Make no mistake, there will be difficult times. However, when you match your goals with a purpose, you get that push you need to go the extra mile. Put structures in place to help you gain the skills necessary to achieve your goals. Structures, in this case, mean anything and anyone that should be a part of this process. For example, what courses must you take? Do you need a mentor? Which skills must you acquire along the way to get to your desired skill level? Put timelines to these structures and have a mechanism in place for accountability.

As far as learning is concerned, there are lots of free and affordable resources online that you can count on. LinkedIn Learning, Udemy, and Coursera are common examples from which you can learn about different topics. Don't stop there, look for professional certifications that validate your skills and knowledge in the desired areas.

Professional certifications are a good idea because they boost your credibility. Your customers and clients feel more confident doing business with someone who knows their stuff, which is also a good thing for your career growth. Be on the lookout for relevant conferences, seminars, and workshops in the industry, because these are usually a good place to network and expand your knowledge on key events and issues in the industry. The beauty of life is that it's a journey of continuous learning, unlearning, and re-learning. If you commit to this process, you're setting yourself on a path to productivity and efficiency. No one has the ultimate monopoly on knowledge. What you know today might not be relevant tomorrow, and that's why we talk about continuous learning and skill development. Once you commit to the pursuit of knowledge, nothing will stand in your way.

Work-Life Balance

Don't lose yourself in the pursuit of success. This is something many entrepreneurs struggle with. When you focus on the goal so much, there's always a risk of getting carried away and losing yourself in the process. Sure, success is the end goal, but if you don't go after it the right way, you might ruin your life in the process.

Fatigue and burnout are common side effects of success. We've seen a lot of people push themselves so hard that they lose sight of the most important piece of the puzzle—themselves! What's the point of working so hard, only to spend most of your money on hospital bills? Even if you're working to create an amazing future for your kids, the effort becomes futile if you are never present.

Now more than ever, the conversation about work-life balance must take center stage, especially when you look at how different fabrics of society are interwoven. Thanks to advancements in technology, we can do so much within a short time. For example, you could start and manage several side hustles while keeping your main job, going to school, and so on. While for most people, this is a good thing, it also raises the problem of not having time for yourself or your loved ones.

As much as you're working towards financial freedom, you must be careful not to get so caught up that you suffer burnout in the process. Whatever you are working on, do not immerse yourself in the business so much to the point where your personal life takes a back seat. You can always find a balance, such that you have time for your responsibilities to yourself as much as those important to your business. At the end of the day, your family, friends, leisure, and other aspects of your personal life still matter. This is an important part of self-care, and a balanced approach will make it easier for you to find fulfillment both in your business or work and outside of it.

Work-life balance is necessary for your overall well-being, job satisfaction, and productivity. It helps prevent stress and exhaustion, making it an important part of your long-term success. It's not even something difficult to accomplish. You just need to be intentional about it. For example, why don't you start by creating clear, healthy boundaries? Decide when your work ends, and stop thinking about work from that point onwards.

If you're working with a team, make sure everyone knows your boundaries, and encourage them to set theirs too. This creates an environment of shared responsibility where you look out for each other and encourage one another to keep a healthy balance between work and your lives. Your work hours should be clear, not just for your team, but for your customers too. Make this visible on your website and social media pages, so anyone who reaches out when you're not working understands that they will not get a response until your working hours begin the next day. This is also a good way to manage customer expectations so that you don't come off as an ignorant, or snobbish business. It might seem difficult at times but try and avoid working beyond your scheduled hours to ensure you have ample time for personal activities.

Most people today work from home, or on a hybrid working module that allows them flexible work hours. If you're working on such a model, you need a dedicated workspace at home. A dedicated workspace sets a clear mental boundary between your work and personal life. You know that when you get into that space, it's all about work. Even your family knows that.

Once you get out of the workspace, it's time for relaxation. You spend time with your family, or do whatever makes you happy, as long as you're not going back to work again. If you have a spare room dedicated to office work, turn off the lights. Mentally, this can also help you condition your body to shut off work mode. Remember, your home office should be strictly for work.

If you're working remotely, be careful not to overwork yourself. This is a common challenge that many people experience in remote working setups. The comfort in your home and the freedom to work when you want has seen many people work long hours at night, or try to accomplish so much within a short period. This is also how burnout creeps into your lifestyle.

Time management will go a long way in helping you keep things in check. Use time management techniques, such as prioritizing tasks, creating to-do lists, and working with deadlines. The point of time management is to encourage you to work smart, not hard. Don't push yourself too hard that you end up overloading your system. Look for ways to make your work more efficient. For example, instead of taking on too many responsibilities, why don't you delegate some roles? You can't always do everything on your own—that's the easiest way to fatigue and burnout. Besides, there's nothing wrong with asking for help, it's not a sign of weakness either.

Know when to ask for help. Don't fall into the trap of trying to do everything on your own. This is about more than just delegating tasks but reaching out to people who are better placed to offer guidance. If you know someone who's achieved what you're working towards, reach out to them and find out how they handled some of the challenges you're experiencing. Talk to a therapist when you feel like you're not in the right frame of mind. At times all it takes is someone with a different or even a radical perspective to help you get through a difficult patch.

Ultimately, work-life balance and your success come down to how well you cultivate the relationships that matter. This is your reminder that your success isn't just about you. There are lots of people whose input will help you get closer to your goals. Your friends, family members, and colleagues have a direct role to play in your pursuit of success.

They might not be directly involved in running your business or advancing your career, but their emotional support and encouragement will always be valuable in your journey. Besides, when you share your experiences with them, you get different perspectives from people who wish you well and can hold you accountable.

Finally, to reiterate the point we made earlier, always think long-term. Everything from your schedule flexibility, stress management techniques, physical activities, and even eating healthy should be built around a long-term plan. Go for those small wins, and build on that energy to pursue your ultimate goals. Don't be afraid to lose or fail. Failure is an important part of success. If anything, failure teaches you how to handle pressure and bounce back stronger.

Conclusion

When you're used to doing things a certain way, switching to something else might not be the easiest thing to do. This is because you've built your life around certain structures and schedules, so switching to something new becomes a problem. We are habitual beings, so it's understandable that some habits might be difficult to drop, just like a bad habit.

Let's flip the script a bit. Everything you've done so far has gotten you this far, but you realize that you are not reaching your potential, and for that reason, you're missing out on big opportunities. In such a scenario, the smartest thing to do is step out of your comfort zone and challenge your thought process. This has been the discussion throughout this book, challenging yourself to do things differently, conquer your money mindset, and aim for greatness.

While changing from your conventional approach to life can be difficult, it can also be the beginning of an exciting journey. For example, think about how a different approach to finances could transform the way you make money and support your loved ones. It's amazing when you think of all the opportunities that could come your way.

Most people are stuck in the nine-to-five mindset, and while it wouldn't be right to begrudge their choices, a new money mindset could reshape their lives financially. This is the core concept of this book. You cannot achieve financial success by following the same flawed approach throughout. Some of the limiting beliefs we have about money are down to conditioning, or the kind of environment in which we were raised.

If you grow up around people who constantly remind you that "money is the root of all evil," it's hard to see it as anything other than trouble. On the other hand, you could look at money as a resource, and what you can do with it. If you take this approach, you'll realize that we are all responsible for our actions, and money has nothing to do with it. If anything, with the right amount of money and a good plan, most of those who spread the gospel of "money being the root of all evil" would be much better off in life.

Real, sustainable change in your finances starts with rethinking your approach to money. Your mindset is one of the most powerful things, so if you can change your perspective of money, you can change your pursuit of it. While it's impossible to guarantee you success, our discussions throughout this book outlined actionable steps you can take to gradually transform your financial story.

With any new project you undertake, there will be challenges. Don't avoid them. Meet them head-on and learn from them. Challenges are unique opportunities to not just learn from your mistakes, but also to build your resilience, and adapt.

Financial freedom is something I believe we all strive for in life. It also means something different for each one of us. For example, my version of financial independence might be taking my family on a vacation, while yours might be living debt-free. Someone else's version might be buying a house and putting all their kids through school without them needing student loans.

Therefore, whatever your reasons, financial independence is a personal matter, and achieving it carries a different sense of personal fulfillment for everyone. You're planning for your future, so it's only right to encourage you to take a futuristic view of money. The future of work and money is already being rewritten, and the foundation lies in flexibility, innovation, and continuous learning. The traditional nine-to-five might not cut it anymore. This doesn't mean you should quit altogether, but instead, explore other options. A single source of income can never get you to success. This is something we see all the time with successful entrepreneurs. They have diversified their investments into different industries, and so should you.

Diversification remains a crucial part of your transition from your nine-to-five to flexible online income. It's not just in spreading your risks across different industries, but also diversification in your thought process. As you set up multiple businesses online, you'll realize that what works for one business might not always work for the others. Some strategies might cut across, but given the unique nature of each business and industry, you will need to reinvent some from time to time. For this to work, you must be adaptable to change. Change is not just inevitable, it is everywhere. The switch from a nine-to-five to setting up multiple online businesses is a sign of change. Change isn't easy, but you have to adapt and get things done. The online business ecosystem evolves so rapidly that you must learn to adjust to emerging trends and new technologies. This is how you remain competitive and relevant in whichever industry you invest in.

The beauty of online business is that you're investing in a platform with lots of opportunities for work and collaboration. As you identify and pursue various opportunities relevant to your goals, interests, and skills, remember that it's just as important to build a personal brand. A strong personal brand makes you stand out and could be the key to attracting new opportunities. People don't just want to know about your company, they also want to know who you are and what you stand for. This is particularly true on social media—people generally believe they can hold you accountable when they can reach and engage you personally rather than through your business. Apart from accountability, a touch of personality also makes your brand more accessible and relatable.

Finally, as you tap into the opportunities that come your way, remember that the online business landscape presents challenges just as much as it presents opportunities. When things aren't going your way, don't throw in the towel. Embrace the challenges with a proactive and open mind, learn from them, adapt, and grow. Sustainable long-term success is a lifelong experience. Invest in acquiring new skills, growing your networks, and looking for opportunities to grow your business interests and personal growth.

Spare a few minutes to reflect on your learning and how it applies to your career goals. Come up with a plan on how to integrate these lessons into your strategies, and set actionable goals for your transition from the trappings of your nine-to-five. Financial independence comes down to your resilience, adaptability, and commitment to lifelong learning.

Remember, the future of work will require more than just surviving change, you must also learn how to thrive in it.

Thank you for purchasing my book and delving into your money mindset. I hope this book helps guide you in your path to the many online income opportunities. Please take a few minutes and leave a review of my book where you purchased it. I would greatly appreciate it. Thank you!

References

Ahead for Business. (2024). *Tackling Small Business Burnout*. Ahead for Business; https://aheadforbusiness.org.au/resources/tackling-small-business-burnout#:~:text=Signs%20and%20symptoms&text=Feelings%20of%20energy%20depletion%20or

Ali, R. (2023, December 22). *4 Steps to Creating a Financial Plan for Your Small Business*. Oracle NetSuite. https://www.netsuite.com/portal/resource/articles/financial-management/small-business-financial-plan.shtml

Blakely-Gray, R. (2022, November 3). *Money Management Tips to Keep Your Small Business in Shape*. Patriot Software. https://www.patriotsoftware.com/blog/accounting/small-business-money-management-tips/

Cantero-Gomez, P. (2022, October 12). *Basic Structure Of A Business Plan For Beginners*. Forbes. https://www.forbes.com/sites/palomacanterogomez/2019/07/24/basic-structure-of-a-business-plan-for-beginners/?sh=3d4992bd2ad3

Carter, R. (2021, April 27). *Could "Entrepreneurial Outsourcing" Be Your Perfect Lazy Way To Make a Great Second Income From…*. Medium. https://roycarter-89394.medium.com/could-entrepreneurial-outsourcing-be-your-perfect-lazy-way-to-make-a-great-second-income-from-15847cfd9453

Cote, C. (2022, March 17). *How to Do Market Research for a Startup*. HBS Online. Business Insights Blog.

https://online.hbs.edu/blog/post/how-to-do-market-research-for-a-startup

Curtis, G. (2024, April 25). *Simple Ways to Keep Your Business Going in Hard Times*. Investopedia. https://www.investopedia.com/articles/pf/09/keep-small-business-afloat.asp

DeMarco, J., & Anthony, L. (2021, June 4). *Startup Funding: What It Is and How to Get Capital for a Business*. NerdWallet. https://www.nerdwallet.com/article/small-business/startup-funding

FasterCapital. (2024). *Expanding Product or Service Offerings*. FasterCapital. https://fastercapital.com/startup-topic/Expanding-Product-or-Service-Offerings.html#:~:text=Expanding%20product%20or%20service%20offerings%20is%20a%20crucial%20strategy%20for

Freedman, M. (2018, May 21). *10 Tips for Managing Small Business Finances*. Business News Daily. https://www.businessnewsdaily.com/5954-smb-finance-management-tips.html

Haan, K. (2024, April 7). *How To Start A Business In 11 Steps (2024 Guide)*. Forbes. https://www.forbes.com/advisor/business/how-to-start-a-business/

Hoffower, H. (2019, February 10). *How to build long-term wealth through passive income and outsourcing*. Business Insider.

https://www.businessinsider.com/financial-freedom-book-passive-income-outsourcing-build-wealth-2019-2?r=US&IR=T

Jhajharia, S. (2023, April 19). *The Benefits of Strategic Partnerships for Scaling your Business*. Growth Idea. https://growthidea.co.uk/blog/the-benefits-of-strategic-partnerships-for-scaling-your-business

Kopp, C. M. (2022, October 2). *What Is Brand Awareness? Definition, How It Works, and Strategies*. Investopedia. https://www.investopedia.com/terms/b/brandawareness.asp

Live And Learn Consultancy. (2013, March 22). *5 Basic Sales Tips for Beginners*. Live And Learn Consultancy. https://www.liveandlearnconsultancy.co.uk/top-10-best-sales-tips-for-success/

Madden, T. (2024, February 2). *The Small Business Owner's Guide to Resilience*. Inc.com. https://www.inc.com/inc-masters/the-small-business-owners-guide-to-reillience.html#:~:text=Building%20resilience%20takes%20on going%20work

MBO Partners. (2023, May 5). *10 Legal Requirements for Starting a Small Business*. MBO Partners. https://www.mbopartners.com/blog/how-start-small-business/legal-requirements-for-starting-a-small-business/

Miller, D. (2024, May 28). *5 Innovative Ways to Run a More Efficient Small Business*. SCORE. https://www.score.org/resource/blog-post/5-innovative-ways-run-a-more-efficient-small-business

Morrison, S. (2019, January 28). *11 Things to Do Before Starting a Business*. Business News Daily; businessnewsdaily.com.

https://www.businessnewsdaily.com/1484-starting-a-business.html

Palmetto Payroll. (2022, September 15). *How to Overcome Small Business Setbacks.* Palmetto Payroll Solutions. https://palmettopayroll.net/how-to-overcome-small-business-setbacks/

Patel, B. (2024, March 27). *7 Smart Small Business Tax Planning Strategies to Help You Save Money.* OnDeck. https://www.ondeck.com/resources/high-value-tax-strategies-for-small-business-owners

Porteous, C. (2020, March 18). *A Beginner's Guide to Small-Business Structures.* Entrepreneur. https://www.entrepreneur.com/starting-a-business/a-beginners-guide-to-small-business-structures/347246

Qualtrics. (n.d.). *How to Increase Brand Awareness: 10 Top Strategies.* Qualtrics. https://www.qualtrics.com/experience-management/brand/how-to-increase-brand-awareness/

Rainey, J. (2023, August 25). *Navigating Burnout as a Small Business Owner: Tips for Getting Back on Track.* Jennarainey.com. https://jennarainey.com/navigating-burnout-as-a-small-business-owner-tips-for-getting-back-on-track/

RingCentral. (2022, March 24). *The future of small businesses: What you need to know.* RingCentral Blog.

https://www.ringcentral.com/us/en/blog/future-of-small-businesses/

Savva, S. (2024, March 25). *14 tips to manage stress as a small business owner*. Waveapps.com. https://www.waveapps.com/blog/managing-stress-as-a-business-owner

Singh, S. (2024, February 19). *Council Post: Unlocking The Secrets Of Successful Entrepreneurs: Passion Versus Prudence*. Forbes. https://www.forbes.com/sites/forbesbusinesscouncil/2024/02/13/unlocking-the-secrets-of-successful-entrepreneurs-passion-versus-prudence/?sh=1f45a2487c65

Small Business Coach. (2024, February 13). *How To Scale Your Small Business Into Something Much Bigger*. Small Business Coach. https://www.smallbusinesscoach.org/how-to-scale-your-small-business-into-something-much-bigger/#:~:text=Setting%20Clear%20Goals%20and%20Objectives&text=Define%20your%20vision%20for%20growth

TechnoServe. (2021, October 28). *Five Reasons to be Excited for the Future of Small Business %*. TechnoServe. https://www.technoserve.org/blog/five-reasons-to-be-excited-for-the-future-of-small-business/

Xeinadin. (2024, February 1). *Strategies for Effective Debt Management in Small Businesses*. Xeinadin.

https://xeinadin.com/blog/strategies-for-effective-debt-management-in-small-businesses/

Image References

Alehandra13. (2018, March 18). *Notes Notebook Coffee* [Image]. Pixabay.com. https://pixabay.com/photos/notes-notebook-coffee-office-3236566/

D4rkwzd. (2021, December 4). *Download Transition, Transformation, Education* [Image]. Pixabay.com. https://pixabay.com/vectors/transition-transformation-education-6838185/

Elegant_Inspiration_Art. (2022, November 5). *Download Problem Solving, Thinking, Process* [Image]. Pixabay.com.

https://pixabay.com/illustrations/problem-solving-thinking-process-7570458/

Franz26. (2023, September 11). *Download Ai Generated, Sunset, Adventure* [Image]. Pixabay.com. https://pixabay.com/illustrations/ai-generated-sunset-adventure-8243562/

Geralt. (2016, August 5). *Download Board, Money, Earn* [Image]. Pixabay.com. https://pixabay.com/illustrations/board-money-earn-work-merit-1572084/

Geralt. (2017, September 9). *Problem Solution Help* [Image]. Pixabay.com. https://pixabay.com/photos/problem-solution-help-support-2731501/

Geralt. (2019, March 12). *Work Process To Organize* [Image]. Pixabay.com. https://pixabay.com/photos/work-work-process-to-organize-4051777/

Geralt. (2019, May 26). *Download Digital Marketing, Product, Contents* [Image]. Pixabay.com. https://pixabay.com/illustrations/digital-marketing-product-contents-4229637/

Geralt. (2021, December 8). *Download Board, Business, Idea* [Image]. Pixabay.com. https://pixabay.com/illustrations/board-business-idea-growth-6853001/

Geralt. (2024, May 22). *Download Ai Generated, Woman, Skills* [Image]. Pixabay.com. https://pixabay.com/illustrations/ai-generated-woman-skills-success-8774131/

GraphicMama-team. (2016, June 15). *Download Presentation, Statistic, Boy* [Image]. Pixabay.com.

https://pixabay.com/vectors/presentation-statistic-boy-1454403/

Kaboompics. (2015, May 31). *Working Female Work* [Image]. Pixabay.com. https://pixabay.com/photos/working-female-work-desk-office-791849/

Mohamed_hassan. (2017, October 11). *Download Multitasking, Efficiency, Time Management* [Image]. Pixabay.com. https://pixabay.com/illustrations/multitasking-efficiency-2840792/

Mohamed_hassan. (2021, December 27). *Download Impossible, Possible, Attitude* [Image]. Pixabay.com. https://pixabay.com/vectors/impossible-possible-attitude-6890980/

Muhammadrizkyklinsman. (2020, May 18*). Download Collection, Brand, Cosmetics* [Image]. Pixabay.com. https://pixabay.com/illustrations/collection-brand-cosmetics-business-5180255/

OpenClipart-Vectors. (2016, March 31). *Download Business, Commerce, Decision*s [Image]. Pixabay.com. https://pixabay.com/vectors/business-commerce-decisions-1297332/

Pexels. (2016, November 29). *Concept Man Papers* [Image]. Pixabay.com. https://pixabay.com/photos/concept-man-papers-person-plan-1868728/

Talhakhalil007. (2019, June 19). *Download Email, Email Marketing, Newsletter* [Image]. Pixabay.com.

https://pixabay.com/vectors/email-email-marketing-newsletter-4284157/

Tumisu. (2022, February 11). *Problem Solution Idea* [Image]. Pixabay.com. https://pixabay.com/photos/problem-solution-idea-creativity-7004146/

U_q203w9nb8g. (2024, July 22). *Digital Marketing Branding Brand* [Image]. Pixabay.com. https://pixabay.com/photos/digital-marketing-branding-8907752/

www.ingramcontent.com/pod-product-compliance
Lightning Source LLC
Chambersburg PA
CBHW071515220526
45472CB00003B/1038